IS... discover

a gift.

—Eliana Light,
singer-songwriter

expressing your ideas in a fun way that entertains.

—Jordan B. "Gorf" Gorfinkel,
author of PASSOVER HAGGADAH GRAPHIC NOVEL

collaboration. Whether it's collaborating with my ancestors, with other food professionals or other writers, whatever I'm working on has a collaborative element to it.

—Jeffrey Yoskowitz, co-founder of The Gefilteria and co-author of THE GEFILTE MANIFESTO

innovation.

—Siona Benjamin,
artist

surprising. It's like when you are just chilling out and you're not purposely trying to be creative that's when the moment hits you. I'm always surprised when I'm just walking down the street and I see a fire truck and a melody just comes into my head.

—Sarah Aroeste, Ladino singer-songwriter

exploration. Pushing the boundary of normal. Creating the unknown.

—Alana Chandler,
author of
TZEVAYIM

coming into the full expression of yourself.

—Rabbi Susan Freeman, dancer with Avodah Dance Ensemble & co-author of TORAH IN MOTION

taking risks.

—Harriete Estel Berman,
artist

the source of everything. Everything comes from someone sitting down and thinking of a new way of going about the world. A new approach, a new way of thinking. Someone once asked, "What if I took two knives and I put them this way?" and invented scissors.

—Hillel Smith, artist

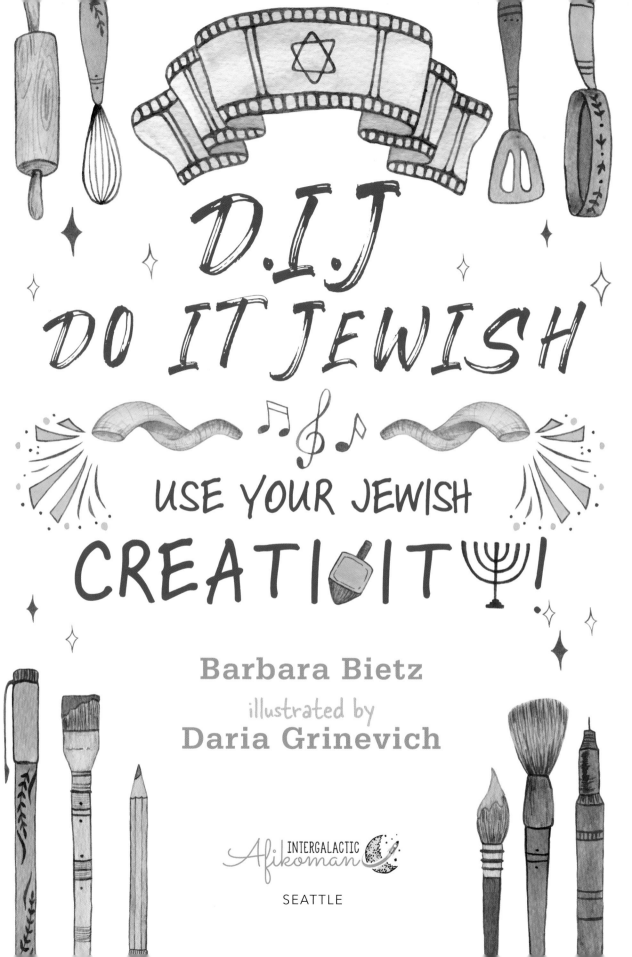

D.I.J
DO IT JEWISH

USE YOUR JEWISH
CREATIVITY!

Barbara Bietz

illustrated by
Daria Grinevich

INTERGALACTIC
Afikoman

SEATTLE

To JB, For all your support
To TB, For keeping it real
Much love, always —BB

For Benny, my love and support —DG

For permission requests, write to the publisher at the address below:

Intergalactic Afikoman
1037 NE 65th Street, #167
Seattle, WA 98115

www.IntergalacticAfikoman.com

Publisher's Cataloging-In-Publication Data

Names: Bietz, Barbara, author. | Grinevich, Daria, illustrator.
Title: D.I.J., do it Jewish : use your Jewish creativity! / Barbara Bietz ; illustrated by Daria Grinevich.
Other Titles: DIJ, do it Jewish | Do it Jewish
Description: First edition. | [Seattle, Washington] : Intergalactic Afikoman, [2020] | Interest age level: 008-012. | Summary: "Learn from Jewish creativity mentors and use your own Jewish creativity in areas ranging from Jewish cooking to Jewish filmmaking"--Provided by publisher.
Identifiers: ISBN 9781951365042 | ISBN 9781951365059 (ebook)
Subjects: LCSH: Creative ability--Juvenile literature. | Jewish cooking--Juvenile literature. | Jewish art--Juvenile literature. | Jewish literature--Juvenile literature. | Authorship--Juvenile literature. | Motion pictures--Production and direction--Juvenile literature. | CYAC: Creative ability. | Jewish cooking. | Jewish art. | Jewish literature. | Authorship. | Motion pictures--Production and direction.
Classification: LCC BM729.C74 B54 2020 (print) | LCC BM729.C74 (ebook) | DDC 296.7--dc23

Library of Congress Control Number: 2020945937
Printed in the USA
2 4 6 8 10 9 7 5 3 1
First Edition

CONTENTS

JEWISH FILMMAKING

GETTING STARTED

"I think everyone has stories to tell. Everyone has a unique perspective," says filmmaker Rachel Harrison Gordon.

Have you wondered what it takes to create a Jewish film? Maybe you've been interested in making a Jewish film but you didn't know how to get started.

Rachel has some ideas. She is the creator of a short film called *Broken Bird*. The film follows a biracial girl named Birdie as she prepares for her bat mitzvah and balances the love and loyalty of her divorced parents.

Broken Bird is based on Rachel's own life experience. Growing up, Rachel loved watching movies and says they "helped her understand what was going on" in her life. "I think that art is one of the best tools that we have for processing, for creating empathy," Rachel shares.

Rachel's loving grandmother encouraged her to write and do art projects. Rachel even had a poem published in a magazine.

In school and in her previous career, Rachel excelled in math and science. But in her heart, she was a storyteller. Still, her path to becoming a filmmaker was unexpected.

At first, Rachel planned to pursue the business side of filmmaking. But then, in graduate school, she had the opportunity to create a film for a class assignment. She realized, "I'm an artist and this is where I should be."

It was not an easy decision to use her own life story for her film. But, Rachel said she "had a hard time not thinking about it." Although she was concerned about creating a film that was so deeply personal, the risks paid off. "It was really cool to see how many people related to it… which was surprising."

If you are interested in making a Jewish film, Rachel says to think about the story first. "Take an experience from your life and just tell your story through a film." Focus on the story and don't be "overwhelmed at the kind of technical aspects" of creating your film.

Where Do You Start with Ideas for a Jewish Film?

While creating *Broken Bird*, Rachel asked herself questions about her own identity, which she hoped to explore in the film. "What does my Blackness mean to me?" "What does my Judaism mean to me?" These questions helped her craft Birdie's storyline for *Broken Bird*.

Rachel says you can ask yourself questions, such as:

* What about my family made me laugh?
* What about my family made me cry?
* What about this day at Hebrew school made me run to the bathroom and hide?
* Think about your own Jewish life. What experiences can you build a a story around?

DOING IT JEWISH

Rachel shares how she was able to incorporate her Jewish identity into *Broken Bird*.

"I feel very proud and grateful to be Jewish," Rachel says.

She was excited to choose a Torah portion for Birdie. "We selected one which was the most relevant for her." The portion she chose was Matot, which explains the importance of honoring the vows that you make and keeping your promises. In the film Birdie invites her dad to her bat mitzvah, without knowing if he will actually come. The theme was perfect for Birdie.

For Rachel, Judaism is about "love and acceptance and community and traditions." Despite some challenging times in her own Jewish community, where she didn't always feel comfortable, Rachel's cantor became her life-long ally. She gave Rachel the message that "I'm good enough, I'm special and I deserve to be here. And I think outside of Hebrew school, she left a lasting impact that I [was] a valid human being."

Rachel's cantor was on the set when Birdie's bat mitzvah scenes were filmed, at the same synagogue where Rachel had her bat mitzvah. Having her cantor's support made the experience even more meaningful.

"Judaism for me has been about humor, and I think it makes a lot of sense as a Jewish people to have humor and to be resilient that way… So that excites me… to communicate subjects that are a little tricky or maybe even heartbreaking but seeing the lightness in it."

–Rachel Harrison Gordon

KEEPING IT GOING

Once you have an idea for your Jewish film, it's time to bring your story to life. First, think about your main character (like Birdie). Rachel says, "Pick a moment in time where that person will experience a journey."

The most important thing to remember, Rachel says, is "What does this film mean to me?" Write it down and don't forget it! advises Rachel. "Put it on a Post-it!"

Before you write your script, Rachel suggests asking yourself questions about your character's journey:

* How does the person change?
* Why do we following that person on that day?
* Why now? Why does [your character] want to do something about it on this day?
* Your character's journey is the story you are telling through film. What will your character's journey be?

MAKING IT AS GOOD AS IT CAN BE

There are a lot of elements to consider before you start filming, like writing the script, casting the actors, and finding props for your set.

Your script is your character's journey in detail. But don't be afraid to "Turn that formula on its head," with an unexpected ending. Rachel says to think of your script as "beats you have to get through," along with "plot points that you need to create a whole [storyline] that makes sense."

You will need to find actors to cast in your film, but you don't need to hire professionals! Your friends and your family members might enjoy being part of your cast. Rachel started casting even before her script was finalized. She says your actors can help you see the roles differently. While you know every line in your script and have an idea of how you will film each scene, you need to be flexible once you get started with casting. "Because you plan and God laughs," Rachel says with a smile.

Once you choose a place where you will film, you can fill your space with props. The props you use on your set will add insight into your characters. Even though not every detail of the film actually happened in Rachel's life, most of the props in Birdie's room come from Rachel's childhood home.

Rachel says, "The most important things were the Black symbols, and they were all adapted from my life." She continues, "I wanted it to be known that there was an effort to incorporate this identity."

If you look closely in Birdie's room, you can see an Alvin Ailey poster. Rachel says, "My mom used to take me to see Alvin Ailey *Revelations* almost every year. And that was a huge inspiration to me… I learned about Black history and Black spirituals." Another personal touch, Rachel says, was "my American Girl doll. She had a little cameo."

In *Broken Bird*, different types of music reflect Birdie's identity. Music is very personal for Rachel. She says, "When you don't have the words to communicate, you often go to other artists, and that's what my dad and I did specifically with music. So I definitely wanted to pay homage to that."

The first scene in Broken Bird shows Birdie practicing her Torah portion. Moments later, we hear Nina Simone singing a classic Hebrew song, "Eretz Zavat Chalav U'dvash" (Land of Milk and Honey). When she first heard this version of the song, Rachel knew it would be perfect for her film. First, "milk and honey sound delicious!" She adds, "This is the optimistic view I'm in search of, a world where there's this harmony between these two things… that's exactly what the story is about."

In another scene, Birdie and her dad listen to "Bad Girls" by Donna Summer in the car. Later, she plays a record of the same song at home, in her mom's house. Rachel says, "This whole sequence was very much autobiographical."

What kinds of music and props would enhance your Jewish film?

The Good and the Bad

It's normal to deal with doubts, Rachel assures us. "There were weeks where I just thought [*Broken Bird*] was not unique or worth capturing."

Getting feedback from the right people is important. Find your creative community, advises Rachel, people you trust. "Find people that are invested in you because people will offer solutions to problems they see in your story."

Rachel gathered a cast and crew of supportive, generous people who helped make the filming of *Broken Bird* a meaningful experience.

"Find your peers that are willing to learn as you're learning," she says. Your creative friends can be "part of the ride." Just like Rachel found her professional team, you can gather your friends and family to be your cast, crew, set designers, and more. There will be a job for everyone!

The Tools You Need

Does it need to cost a lot of money to make your Jewish film?

"A lot of people are intimidated by it because they feel like it's going to require a big investment and it's not necessarily the case," Rachel says.

You can use a phone to shoot your Jewish film. "Sound is actually more important than visuals," Rachel says. "Invest in a good microphone."

That's all the technology you need to make a Jewish film—your phone and a microphone!

When it's time to edit your film, there are computer programs and apps you can use on your phone. Rachel explains, "The film programs work like word processing programs that you can save a version, make changes, but still save the old version [or] what they used to call 'the cutting room floor.'" Just in case you change your mind.

The first step in editing is called an "assembly cut." Rachel explains, "Just edit it together in the order that you wrote it." This may be enough for a beginning filmmaker.

TAKING IT FURTHER

For Rachel, it was essential that *Broken Bird* featured authentic Jewish details.

While filming, Rachel realized she didn't have a copy of Birdie's Torah portion that was the right size for the camera. Rachel thought, "No one will notice if the Hebrew is wrong, but… that was what kept me up at night… And it mattered to me."

It was important to Rachel that the process be authentic and comfortable for the actors, too. Rachel asked her cantor to record the Torah portion for Indigo Hubbard-Salk, the actor who played Birdie. "I wanted her to have a legitimate teacher," Rachel says. After playing the role of Birdie, Indigo decided to have her own bat mitzvah.

Making a Jewish film can be an exciting process. If you focus on the story you want to tell, as Rachel advises, you will be proud of what you create.

Rachel is proud of the Jewish film she created.

"Just the fact that our film exists and now there's an image of a Black woman holding a Torah on the bema… And that's just our contribution to the world. And that fills me with joy."

| *What is your Jewish film going to share with the world?*

Rachel Harrison Gordon is a storyteller and data analyst. She has a degree in engineering from the University of Pennsylvania and was a Presidential Innovation Fellow. Among other accolades, Rachel was selected as a member of NASA's Datanauts. She has also worked in film production.

Rachel is the creator of the acclaimed film, Broken Bird.

"WHEN YOUR 11-YEAR-OLD KID ASKS TO MAKE A DOCUMENTARY FILM WITH YOU, THE ANSWER IS 'YES! YES! YES!'"

— Peter Miller, director of *Egg Cream*

"When I was 11, my dad and I were talking about what he did for work," says Nora Claire Miller. "And we thought, wouldn't it be great if we came up with a movie?"

Nora and her dad, filmmaker Peter Miller, began working on a film together.

Years later, Nora, Peter, and film editor Amy Linton finished that film.

"I was in a creative Hebrew school," explains Nora, that encouraged "asking questions and then pursuing those questions in creative ways." Nora's teacher, Jerry, taught them about the Talmud and about "rabbis asking each other questions into infinity." Their film, Egg Cream, started with one of Nora's Hebrew school questions, "Where do egg creams come from?"

> *"Imagination and a sense of commitment to telling a good tale is way more important than any piece of technology."—Peter Miller*

STARTING A FILM TOGETHER

"My father grew up in the Jewish ghetto in Boston and we lived in the suburbs," says Peter, "so drinking an egg cream was a way of looking at his past and the world that he had come from."

"Then I was lucky enough to have kids," says Peter, "and one of the greatest joys in the world was introducing my kids to egg creams."

So when Nora asked about the origin of the egg cream and if she could join him in making a documentary, they decided to make a film about the egg cream.

Nora and Peter started traveling all around New York City asking people about egg creams. They spent a couple of years "going places, drinking egg creams and having Nora ask open-ended questions."

"The kinds of curiosity that Nora had, the questions she asked, were the kinds of qualities that make for a great filmmaker," says Peter. "I think we could bring kids along more often on our projects and they would come out differently and better in some ways."

FUN FACT:
Nora's Hebrew school teacher, Jerry, appears in Egg Cream, *telling an amazing, apocryphal story of how the egg cream came to be.*

"We went digging through old archives and finding every photo that we ever could of egg creams and footage of old soda fountains," says Peter. They even found the only song ever made about the egg cream, by "a wonderful rock star named Lou Reed." Reed's family let them use the song in the film.

They started the film when Nora was 11 and the last day of filming was at Nora's bat mitzvah when she was 13. They served egg creams, of course!

But then Nora lost interest in the project, and a decade passed before father and daughter worked on it together again.

FINISHING THEIR FILM

One day, Peter emailed Nora a video clip of an interview with her and her sister. "We were both standing there… holding the microphones and interviewing each other," says Nora. "I was like wow, there's got to be something here."

Then Amy took the video and edited it into a short piece. Now Nora was able to see "what it could be."

To finish their film, Nora and Peter wrote a script, Nora recorded the voice-over, and Amy edited it.

Amy explains that film editing is "like I have a piece of marble that I can start carving away… and get down to the essence of it."

ADVICE FOR ASPIRING FILMMAKERS

"One of the beautiful things about the technology that we all carry around in our pocket is the ability to record video and make movies," says Peter, but that "doesn't mean it's easy to tell a good story."

"At the heart of all filmmaking is storytelling," he emphasizes.

To make your Jewish film, Peter advises you to find an important topic and then think about "where the stories live in that subject."

"How can you… make it into a narrative," asks Peter, "[that] takes you on a journey where you feel emotions and suspense… and want to know what's going to happen next and where… you've learned something that touches you inside as a person?"

"What feels so special about *Egg Cream*," says Nora, is that it tells "a very specific story about a very specific facet of Jewish culture… and suddenly you're able to understand something deeper about the Jewish immigrant experience."

- -

Nora's Egg Cream Recipe

1. Take a tall glass ("it shouldn't be a short glass") with about one inch of milk.

2. Then take a spoon and tilt it at a 45-degree angle and take a bottle of seltzer ("which I recently found out some people call sparkling water. But you don't want that. You want seltzer"). Take your seltzer and you pour it over this 45-degree-angle spoon so that it creates a head of foam. That head of foam is pivotally important. Without it, it's not an egg cream. You want the foam to create a large section of froth at the top of the cup. Take your chocolate syrup ("And it should be "Foxes U-Bet. But if you can't get that, any type of chocolate syrup is fine. Never vanilla!) and pour it down the middle of the cup.

3. Take your chocolate syrup ("and it should be Fox's U-Bet. But if you can't get that, any type of chocolate syrup is fine. Never vanilla!") and pour it down the middle of the cup.

4. Then take your spoon and without disturbing the head of foam ("this is the hard part") with this movement of your wrist, move the spoon back and forth. Don't stir it in a big swirl because that will mess up the foam. Create sort of a hinge point ("basically you're trying not to disturb the foam").

5. Then mix up the chocolate syrup with the milk. And at the end, you should have about six inches of brown liquid topped by a couple of inches of foam. This is what Jerry referred to as white fire on black fire, which is what the Torah once was and what the egg cream was too.

DIJ | DO IT JEWISH
FILMMAKING POSSIBILITIES

1. Interview a family member. Create a short video of your interview. If your interview is on the phone, Nora encourages you to take a video of yourself on the phone! "Make art that shows the different ways that we talk to each other."

2. Take your favorite Jewish song and find images for it. Edit it together to create your own music video, suggests Amy.

3. Choose your own Jewish topic to research like Peter and Nora did with egg cream. Who could you interview about your topic? What photos or other resources can you find? Use simple video editing software to put your interviews and research into a short documentary.

4. Take a Jewish experience from your life, like Rachel did in *Broken Bird*, and think through how you can show it in film. Will you write a short script? Recruit friends for actors? Collect the best props possible to tell your unique Jewish story?

FILMMAKING TOOLS:

* a phone or camera
* a good microphone
* paper and pencil or a computer (to write your script
* photo archives
* your best research skills

GLOSSARY

bat mitzvah – a Jewish girl becomes a Jewish adult at the age of twelve or thirteen, the ceremony where this Jewish adulthood is celebrated

bema – the platform in a synagogue where the Torah is read

egg cream – a sweet drink consisting of neither egg nor cream (see recipe)

Matot – a Torah portion in the book of Numbers

Talmud – a collection of writings in which rabbis through generations discuss Jewish law

Torah – sacred Jewish text and scroll, the Hebrew Bible

JEWISH CARTOONING & GRAPHIC NOVELS

GETTING STARTED

Have you ever wondered what it takes to create a Jewish cartoon or graphic novel?

A cartoon or comic can be just a few panels.

Graphic novels, on the other hand, are like longer versions of comic books, including a fully developed story. Like a traditional novel.

Terri Libenson is the creator of both comics and graphic novels. "The Pajama Diaries" is a nationally syndicated newspaper comic strip about a Jewish family. Terri is also the author of a series of graphic novels called Emmie & Friends. One of the most recent graphic novels in Terri's series is called *Becoming Brianna*. In *Becoming Brianna*, Terri tells the story of Brianna, a middle-schooler who has just agreed to have a bat mitzvah. Brianna is a good student, but learning Hebrew is hard! She struggles to balance all the bat mitzvah preparation with family, school, and friends.

Becoming a Cartoonist

Terri always wanted to be an artist. She can't remember a time when she didn't have a pencil in her hand. She loved comics and started creating her own early on. Terri remembers that she "teamed up with another kid on our block and we'd draw pages and pages of comics after school every day."

If you enjoy drawing and storytelling, maybe you could be a cartoonist or a graphic novelist like Terri. To get started, Terri says you don't need expensive tools. While you can use an electronic tablet, there's no need to restrict yourself. "These days, the sky's the limit!" says Terri. Feel free to experiment with all kinds of pens and pencils. When Terri was a kid, she used colored pencils.

Your comic or graphic novel could start with a doodle. Terri recalls her own school days decorating her notebook margins and brown paper bag book covers. "I decorated in doodles," she says. "I couldn't stop."

Terri also encourages would-be graphic novel creators to read. Whether it's picture books, novels, or a big stack of magazines, reading can inspire your own ideas. If you haven't hit on just the right idea, Terri suggests taking a break for an activity you enjoy. Sometimes a change of scenery is all you need. Terri explains that when you are relaxed, whether you are on a bike ride or a walk in the neighborhood, ideas can flow.

When you are ready to get started creating your own Jewish comic or graphic novel, you can brainstorm story ideas, using your own life for inspiration. "Characters can be based on people you know—or even based on you," Terri says.

"I jot down story ideas on a notepad. It's also okay to type ideas into a computer or your phone. Whatever works. I try not to edit myself and just write down ideas until I feel like I have enough."

As the creator of your "graphic novel world," it's up to you. Terri says, "It's a combination of being inspired and then… finding your own voice."

DOING IT JEWISH

Are you wondering how to create characters and a storyline for your Jewish comic or graphic novel?

Terri has advice for you. "Maybe start with your own family," she says. "What does your family do when it comes to Jewish traditions?" Personal family stories and celebrations are always unique and a great place to inspire your Jewish graphic novel. Or what about your own Jewish experience? Think about youth group or religious school, Terri suggests. "There's so much rich material there. That's a perfect jumping-off point."

In her comic "The Pajama Diaries," Terri wanted to show an authentic family—like hers. So she made the family Jewish. During the holidays, "they did what my family did and celebrated Jewish holidays," explains Terri. In the comic, the family fasts on Yom Kippur and gets rid of their chametz for Passover. And, when one of the characters in "Pajama Diaries" turned 13, Terri created bat mitzvah storylines, "which were a lot of fun."

Becoming Brianna is part of the Emmie & Friends series. It is Terri's first specifically Jewish book in the series, all about Brianna's bat mitzvah journey.

Jewish comics and graphic novels can be filled with humorous moments. In *Becoming Brianna*, Brianna's mom is super excited about bat mitzvah planning. Too excited.

In the book, Brianna's mom pulls out two Tootsie Rolls from a bag and announces to Brianna: "I can tie them together with cute ribbons to make them look like little Torahs."

Art by Terri Libenson

Brianna's response: "You've seriously gone off the deep end!"

This fun detail in the book came from Terri's imagination. Terri says, "I was just trying to figure out something goofy for her mom to do." In this short scene, we learn a lot about both characters and their relationship.

In another scene, just as Brianna is getting ready to read from the Torah, her rabbi takes out his cell phone for a bat mitzvah selfie. Huh? That's what Brianna says, too! "It's tradition!" her rabbi explains. "Mitzvah kid takes a selfie with the rabbi. We post it on the temple page."

This selfie scene was inspired by Terri's own Jewish life. "That absolutely happened with both of my kids." She says the selfies help kids feel "a little less nervous." The real selfie-taking rabbi was the inspiration for Brianna's rabbi in the graphic novel.

Your Jewish details can come from your imagination or from your real Jewish life, just like Terri's.

"Write what you love to write or what you love to illustrate. It's going to be more from the heart and more authentic" —Terri Libenson

If you want to add Jewish elements to your work but you have questions, Terri reminds you that you can reach out for help. Terri needed a Torah portion for Brianna to read from for her bat mitzvah. Terri met with one of her own rabbis.

"I knew I needed a portion that was significant for Brianna," explains Terri, "and it had to be at a certain time of the year. So he helped me find the right Torah portion." But, Terri says proudly, "I do take credit for the actual **d'var Torah**." Just like a seventh grader preparing for her own bat mitzvah, Terri had to dig deep to write Brianna's speech.

If you need some extra details to create your Jewish comic or graphic novel, you can find a lot of information in books and online, but don't be afraid to contact a local rabbi, cantor, or Hebrew teacher.

KEEPING IT GOING

There are a lot of ways to approach your Jewish cartoon or graphic novel.

What should you create first—the art or the story?

Terri starts with the story first. She will often write out a few paragraphs she calls an "overview." Terri writes two outlines for each of the characters in these books. (*Becoming Brianna* is told from the perspective of "past Bri" and "present Bri.") Terri explains, "I like to know how the ending's going to be even before I start."

Maybe you'd like to start with your character and drawing scenes. That's okay, but Terri shares that when she was working on her second book, she started by doing the story and illustrating it with rough sketches right away.

And then she had to change the whole story.

Uh-oh! That meant that Terri had to get rid of all her sketches. And start over. "That's when I said there's absolutely no way I'm ever roughing anything out again until I have this story down pat," Terri says with a laugh.

If you do hit a bump in your process, it's okay. Terri suggests stepping away from your work for a while. "It is easy to get overwhelmed or feel stuck with a creative project." When you return, you will see your work with "fresh eyes."

DRAWING TIP FROM TERRI
"Try to find drawing styles you admire and figure out what you like about them. You can even take aspects of them and put them in your own work. Not to copy, but to be sort of a jumping-off point. And to give you some inspiration."

MAKING IT AS GOOD AS IT CAN BE

"Learn to edit," Terri suggests. "That's just as important as writing and drawing." Sometimes, you might need to rewrite a story to get it just right. Terri recalls that she rewrote *Positively Izzy* at least four times.

Terri recommends getting feedback from people you trust. Terri's husband reads her books and so does a good friend, who is also a librarian. Terri explains, though, "mainly it's really just me and my editor. I really trust her. She's really brought me far… [Her feedback] is invaluable."

So maybe you don't have a professional editor—yet. But surely you have friends and family who can give you feedback about your Jewish cartoons and graphic novels.

TAKING IT FURTHER

If you want to take your Jewish cartoons or graphic novel to the next level, "find the process that works for you and [give] it a chance to work," Terry advises.

There is no right or wrong way, emphasizes Terri. "I've honed my skills after a lot of trial and error. You don't get good at something until you try it many, many times."

In Terri's graphic novels, close attention to detail provides a perfect balance of developed characters and Jewish life—which makes for an engaging Jewish cartoon or graphic novel.

Take the scene in *Becoming Brianna* when Brianna questions her rabbi about her Torah portion.

"Something I've wrestled with myself, Bri," the rabbi replies. "Wanna discuss?"

Brianna responds, "Yes!"

Terri loves that Judaism encourages you to discuss and learn more. And Brianna's character "doesn't always just accept that yes-or-no answer about 'why.' That's just her nature." So this scene made sense to Terri because Brianna's interaction with her rabbi was consistent with her character. In this moment, we feel like we know Brianna and her rabbi.

> *What scenes in your cartoon or graphic novel will help your characters feel real?*

Another way you can take your Jewish comic and graphic novel creation to a new level is to find new ways to be inspired by your life or the world around you. Inspiration can come from exploring new ideas. For example, Terri's mom is Sephardic. "The Sephardic side of my family has always fascinated me," Terri shares. "It's a little more unique in this country and I'm actually trying to do some research for a book about the Spanish Inquisition, like a graphic novel. So that's my passion project on the side."

Do you have any interesting family stories or experiences that might inspire you in new ways? Or maybe there is a time or place in Jewish history that interests you? Don't be afraid to explore! It might turn into your own Jewish cartoon or graphic novel.

Jewish comics and graphic novels are a lot of fun to read and even more fun to create. Practice your drawing and writing, and one day you'll be the creator of your own Jewish comic or graphic novel!

Terri Libenson is a New York Times *bestselling children's book author of the middle-grade series* Emmie & Friends *(Balzer + Bray). Her graphic novel* Becoming Brianna *follows Brianna through her bat mitzvah preparation.*

Terri is an award-winning cartoonist of the syndicated daily comic strip "Pajama Diaries," which features a Jewish family. She has also written greeting cards for American Greetings.

Terri has a BFA from Washington University in St. Louis.

"I WISH I HAD THIS WHEN I WAS YOUNGER. A COMIC BOOK THAT YOU CAN READ DURING THE HAGGADAH AND UNDERSTAND WHAT YOU'RE READING.""

– Erez Zadok, illustrator of
Passover Haggadah Graphic Novel

"So if you're going to do a Jewish graphic novel, and you're thinking about what is going to be the most useful and the most popular and the most exciting story to tell, Passover has it all," says Jordan B. "Gorf" Gorfinkel.

"It has a reason to use the graphic novel, not just for reading, but also… for the seder. It has the Exodus story. It has all of Judaism… a little bit of thought [and]… history and archaeology and customs and Jewish law and Jewish tradition. It's everything all wrapped up in one."

But the real challenge, explains Gorf, is how do you take this sprawling book that is a little bit of everything and turn it into a story with a beginning, a middle, and an end?

Gorf and his co-creator, Erez Zadok, took on this enormous challenge when they created the *Passover Haggadah Graphic Novel*.

Long before their collaboration, Gorf and Erez had each been passionate about cartooning.

For Erez, it began with a "girl in kindergarten. I wanted her to like me, so I did the thing I knew

> "I'm passionate about my Judaism, and I like to use cartoons in order to get other people to feel passionate too."
> –Jordan B. "Gorf" Gorfinkel

how to do best. I drew a Ninja Turtle for her, and it worked!"

Gorf was an introverted child who "read a lot of comic books on Shabbat and moved practically every year to another city… [His] only consistent friends from city to city were superheroes."

Erez remembers seeing the movie *The Lion King*. "I was in shock," says Erez. "I decided that's what I'm going to do when I grow up."

Then Erez learned that there was a better and more realistic way for him to tell stories… by using comics! No need to draw 24 frames per second to show a hand moving like in animation. With only one panel in comics, he could tell an entire story.

Eventually, Gorf got a job working on *Batman*. Then he formed a comic company of his own. "The dream was always to combine my two loves, comics and Judaism."

One of Erez's professors at the Bezalel Academy of Arts & Design introduced him to Gorf, who was looking for an illustrator for a graphic novel Haggadah.

TURNING THE HAGGADAH INTO A GRAPHIC NOVEL

"It took all our collective skill… to make this ancient book into a story," says Gorf.

"You can find different Haggadot with beautiful illustrations," says Erez, "but none of them is taking the exact text [of the Haggadah] and turning it into a graphic novel."

Initially, Gorf was the writer and Erez was the artist. But as they got to know each other, the roles became blurred. "[Erez] was as much a writer through his art as I ever could have been," says Gorf.

from Passover Haggadah Graphic Novel
by Jordan B. Gorfinkel and Erez Zadok

Gorf would start by writing the script. Then Erez would take the script and turn it into a layout. This means he took a page and broke it into panels. He would draw these in a quick way.

Then Erez would move on to the penciling stage, where he would include details. "You can see the figures, you can see the balloons, the dialogue, everything. You can read it. But it's without columns."

Finally, after they got the details right, Erez moved on to the inking and coloring stage.

PASSION FOR DETAILS

"Imagination is already baked into Judaism… just read the Talmud. You have amazing flights of fantasy that… help you get deeper into the spiritual aspects of Judaism. For me, that's what comics does. It allows me to understand and to dig deeper into Judaism through a medium that is fun and fantastic."
–Jordan B. "Gorf" Gorfinkel

Erez emphasized that Gorf was passionate about getting those details just right. And when it came to certain details, Gorf and Erez revised them over and over.

Erez and Gorf invite you to create Jewish comics of your own. You just need pen and paper, says Gorf.

"That's the beautiful thing about comics. Just start… doing it. But most importantly, share it with people. Comics is not meant to be something that you keep to yourself."

Finally, Gorf shares an important reminder: "Comics is the combination of words and pictures in order to tell a message from you directly to your audience. So if you can draw a stick figure and you can write words on a page and you can tell a story… you can do comics.

"Don't think of it as an art project. Think of it as a story project."

DIJ | DO IT JEWISH
CARTOONING & GRAPHIC NOVEL POSSIBILITIES

1. Try choosing a scene from a Torah story and turning it into a cartoon. What would your cartoon look like if Noah was loading the animals onto the ark? Or if Moses was speaking to the burning bush?

2. Try taking a scene from your own Jewish life and turning it into a cartoon. Do you want to make a cartoon of your sister's bat mitzvah or building the perfect Purim costume? Your real Jewish life provides plenty of ideas for cartoons.

3. Do you have a longer Jewish story in mind? Try starting your own Jewish graphic novel.

4. Would you like to create a cartoon about another time period in Jewish history? What time period would you like to feature in your cartoon? How will you research that time period and put some of your research in your comic?

CARTOONING & GRAPHIC NOVEL TOOLS:

* paper and pencil
* colored pencils
* ink pens
* your imagination!

GLOSSARY

bat mitzvah – a Jewish girl becomes a Jewish adult at the age of twelve or thirteen, the ceremony where this Jewish adulthood is celebrated

chametz – bread or other leavened food, traditionally not eaten during Passover

d'var Torah – literally "a word of Torah," a speech, often given by the bar or bat mitzvah or the rabbi

Exodus – leaving Egypt when the Israelites were slaves

Haggadah – the book that is traditionally read during the Passover seder

Haggadot – the plural of Haggadah

layout – the arrangement of images and panels on a page

Passover – a Jewish holiday that celebrates the Israelites exodus from Egypt

script – how graphic novelists write out their story

seder – the meal Jews eat on Passover, means "order"

Sephardic – Jews from Spain and their descendants

Talmud – a collection of writings in which rabbis through generations discuss Jewish law

Torah – sacred Jewish text and scroll, the Hebrew Bible

Yom Kippur – Day of Atonement, a Jewish fast day

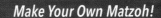

Make Your Own Matzoh!
"It's so easy to do… It tastes better.
The holidays are better. Everyone appreciates it!
And then you can take that matzoh… and make
it into matzoh balls and make your own matzoh
meal… It makes the holidays richer and fuller.
Food… is the vehicle to the deeper meaning."
—Jeffrey Yoskowitz

JEWISH COOKING
CREATING JEWISH RECIPES

GETTING STARTED

Did you ever wonder how and why recipes for your favorite Jewish foods were created? Are you interested in creating Jewish recipes of your own?

For food entrepreneur and writer Jeffrey Yoskowitz, recipes are about more than preparing and cooking food. For Jeffrey, it's the story behind a recipe that makes it meaningful.

Jeffrey's interest in recipes and cooking began with his beloved grandmother's apple strudel. "She cooked it every time she came to visit us in New Jersey. She would bring this apple strudel and all the children would fight over it. And I loved it so much."

When Jeffrey was just eight or nine, he watched his grandma make the strudel and wrote down the recipe. "Ruth's Apple Strudel" is one of the recipes in Jeffrey's book, co-authored with Liz Alpern, *The Gefilte Manifesto*. A photo of his handwritten version, misspellings and all, appears in the book.

Jeffrey and Liz are also the co-founders of The Gefilteria, a food/consulting/ educational company that began as their desire to "to reinvigorate Ashkenazi cuisines." That journey began with gefilte fish. Jeffrey wanted to take this traditional Jewish dish, which some Jews had come to feel ashamed of, and create something that could be enjoyed and celebrated. They have created several different recipes for gefilte fish that are in *The Gefilte Manifesto*.

Are you ready to try your hand at creating a Jewish recipe of your own?

Jeffrey says a good place to start is with cookbooks. He says, "There are some amazing Jewish cookbooks and the cookbooks themselves tell stories. They have beautiful histories, but they also provide context."

Jeffrey's advice is to "look around and see what else is out there. So if there already is a recipe for something you want to make, well, make it, try it, and then figure out what you want to add to it."

How do you make a recipe uniquely yours? Jeffrey says to ask yourself how you can put yourself into a recipe. Think about a flavor your family might enjoy. "Start with learning how to make that classic dish before you start weaving in something new."

"Learn the basics," Jeffrey says. "Then innovate."

What personal "flavors" will you add to your Jewish recipes?

Create A Jewish Recipe Like Jeffrey And Liz

1. Choose a recipe from a Jewish cookbook or use a family recipe.

2. Research the history of the recipe in cookbooks or online. Where did it originate? How have the ingredients changed over time? Is there a meaningful story or symbolism?

3. Make the recipe the traditional way.

4. Change up the recipe using your own creative ideas! Try new spices or other ingredients.

5. Trial and error: Keep trying different combinations until you like what you have created.

6. Share your unique creation with family and friends.

DOING IT JEWISH

So, you want to create a Jewish recipe. Where do you start? Find inspiration from your own life! Start with a story, a memory, or a family tradition.

Stories can play an important role in Jewish recipes. Jeffrey shares his memories of hearing his grandmother's stories, the intertwining of food with storytelling. He has a great-aunt who lives in Israel. Every year she gathers family members in the kitchen to make kreplach for Sukkot. It is a family tradition of gathering, sharing stories, cooking, eating, and celebrating. Through cooking and creating recipes, Jeffrey says he has "connected a lot more to [his] own family's story, connecting more to [his] Jewishness and to Jewish people in other parts of the world."

Do you have family traditions or stories that you can bring to your recipes? Do you want to create a family tradition? Jeffrey says, "A powerful way of engaging or expressing your Jewish identity is in something as simple as cooking Shabbat dinner or cooking for a holiday, cooking with your family… or learning how to make a recipe." He encourages you to create something special for a Shabbat or holiday meal. Take an active role in meal preparation. Maybe your recipe will become part of a new family tradition.

What if you don't see your experiences reflected in a cookbook or traditional recipe? Jeffrey has an idea for you. Let's say you are interested in making blintzes. "Maybe your family is part Ashkenazi and part Moroccan and you want to make a blintz that tells that story. So how can you work in those Moroccan elements? Or maybe you traveled to India and you got inspired by some of these spices. You're working on a classic dish, but you want to weave in something new." Jeffrey says that when a young person creates a recipe and shares it with family, it will become a tradition that gets carried on.

KEEPING IT GOING

Another way you can bring deeper meaning into your Jewish recipes is through research. Jeffrey says, "Recipe inspiration often comes not just from cookbooks. It comes from doing historical research, reading old Yiddish novels, and learning about how people eat and then wanting to reference that in my cooking. Think about what inspires you." He explains that a recipe is a guide for someone to follow and encourages creating recipes that are infused with "story, with soul, with purpose, with voice."

Jeffrey shares some insights about working with his Gefilteria partner, Liz. He says, "We were trying to take older recipes and then breathe a different kind of life into them, add a new spirit to them."

For example, Jeffrey and Liz wanted to create a new recipe for tzimmes, a traditional Rosh Hashanah dish. They did research. "How can we play with using the history of this dish to inform the future of the dish?" Jeffrey asks, then explains, "We wanted to honor the fact that carrots, sliced in a specific way, were made to resemble coins, to be a symbol for prosperity in the new year. We loved that symbolism."

They started by carefully looking at traditional ingredients of tzimmes: "So it's vegetables," says Jeffrey. "It's dried fruit. It's some kind of sweet syrup. Often honey based." Jeffrey and Liz asked themselves, "What can we do with this?" "How can we make sure it still has the spirit of the tzimmes that people love?" Their goal was to create something new, but also "reference the past." Jeffrey describes the process as weaving a story together.

Once they had ideas for their new recipe, it was time to try them out. Jeffrey and Liz worked in separate kitchens, experimented with different vegetables and other ingredients, compared their variations, and even shared them with others. Trial and error is an important part of creating recipes.

MAKING IT AS GOOD AS IT CAN BE

"You have to put the work in," Jeffrey says. "You have to spend time." Once a recipe is ready to go, Jeffrey shares the written recipe with friends. He says, "I would send them a recipe that I had written. And I said, 'Follow the recipe. Exactly. And let me know what I did wrong.'" Getting feedback from others is an important part of the recipe creation process.

When you are preparing and cooking your recipes, having the right tools is also important. Jeffrey says not to worry about fancy gadgets, but a good knife and cutting board are essential. And your hands are the most important tool of all. He also stresses the importance of fresh vegetables, from a local farmer's market or even from your

own garden. "Jewish foods are foods of the home," he says. "If you really want to get to know the history of Jewish cooking, Ashkenazi or other, it's about knowing where food comes from and actually being connected to that."

Ask a Relative

Using tools that have been in your family for many years can make your cooking even more meaningful. Jeffrey's Grandma Ruth gave him some of his favorite tools—a rolling pin, and a chopping blade and bowl. Collect family recipes, too. Talk to your parents and grandparents about their recipes, family traditions, and experiences with Jewish food. Learn from them, and incorporate their stories in your own Jewish recipes and meal prep. Imagine creating a new version of a family recipe, and using your grandparents' tools to help you!

TAKING IT FURTHER

For Jeffrey, preparing a Shabbat meal brings special meaning. When Shabbat candles are lit and a prayer is made over the challah, it means even more because of the effort made in creating, braiding, and baking the challah.

If you want to share your Jewish recipes in a meaningful way, create a meal for your family and friends, or *with* your family and friends. Jeffrey talks about the storytelling that takes place in the kitchen, cooking the foods together. By making and sharing your own Jewish recipes, you are creating stories, traditions, and memories. Maybe for generations to come. Jeffrey calls this "the rhythm of Jewish life."

Find Your Passion — Pickles?

Jeffrey is passionate about pickles. To become an expert pickler, he followed his own advice. Jeffrey spent time on an organic farm. It was there he discovered how to make pickles, in gigantic drums with bushels of cucumbers and dill and garlic. "These pickles were amazing," he shares. And a passion was born. Jeffrey wanted to make pickles on a smaller scale. He recalls: "My first culinary act as a young adult was creating a recipe, but I was actually translating a recipe and then teaching others how to make it, which is where a lot of my inspiration comes."

Go find your passion; whether it's pickles, gefilte fish, tzimmes, blintzes, or another delicious Jewish food, give it your all! Learn as much as you can and keep creating new Jewish recipes and meaningful food experiences.

Jeffrey Yoskowitz is a food entrepreneur, passionate pickler, and food writer. Co-founder of The Gefilteria, he and his partner, Liz Alpern, offer Jewish dining experiences all over the world. Jeffrey is one of the organizers of the Great Big Jewish Food Fest. Jeffrey co-authored The Gefilte Manifesto: New Recipes for Old World Jewish Foods *along with Liz Alpern. His work has been published in numerous magazines and newspapers.*

"I WANTED JEWS OF COLOR TO READ THIS AND REALIZE 'I'M NOT ALONE'..."

— Alana Chandler, author of *Tzevayim*

From doodling on the side of her notebook to creating "elaborate, sometimes odd costumes" for her Jewish day school's Spirit Week, Alana Chandler has always loved being creative.

Since she was a child, Alana has liked baking. "What kid doesn't love dessert?"

But Alana's interest in cooking blossomed her freshman year of high school when she and her friends decided to do weekly potluck-style lunches.

ENCOURAGEMENT FROM ALANA
"I don't want kids to doubt themselves even though they don't have the resume or the professional credentials. I surely don't!"

Alana got "so into it," preparing quiches, macarons, and other elaborate dishes as an excuse to delay doing her homework.

"Hey, you should post this stuff on Instagram!" said a friend. And so Alana's cooking Instagram, "Chow by Chandler," was born.

A POWERFUL INTERNSHIP

During high school, Alana completed a Jewish feminist internship. She spent a year learning about "power, privilege, intersectionality, and other topics with a social justice lens, also examining their intersections with Judaism."

One thing that struck Alana during her internship was that she was the only person who didn't look white.

"It became clear to me over the years that I don't see people who look like me in synagogue often, if at all," says Alana. "Growing up, I felt very out of place in my Jewish school."

For her personal internship project, Alana decided she "wanted to create something that would allow other Jews of color to feel accepted and recognized in the Jewish community."

A COOKBOOK TO MAKE A DIFFERENCE

Alana decided to create a cookbook called Tzevayim, featuring recipes by Jewish women of color from Chicago.

Alana thought food could be a vehicle for understanding cultures. One of Alana's grandfathers speaks Japanese and one speaks English. "Even though they can't communicate, sitting across the table and sharing the same meal, it's camaraderie."

Alana hoped her cookbook could make a difference. "If even one Jew of color could see this, it would make me happy," says Alana.

And she wanted people who aren't Jews of color to read her cookbook and realize that there are many "different identities that define and intersect with Judaism. Just because Jewish people might not be from Israel or Europe doesn't make them any less Jewish."

Alana began by contacting her synagogue. Her cantor helped connect her with Jews of color in the community who were passionate about food. She found others through searching the internet.

Alana was especially excited to reach out to Molly Yeh, a cookbook author, blogger, and Food Network host who is Chinese and Jewish. Molly allowed Alana to include her recipe for scallion pancake challah in *Tzevayim*.

BE A COOKING SCIENTIST

Recently, Alana made a tricolor melon pan challah. She coated the challah in this cookie crust.

One braid was matcha filled with red bean paste, one was a plain challah dough filled with honey butter, and the third was chocolate dough filled with chocolate chips.

Photo by Alana Chandler

> "Some people might think that fusion food is a disgrace to tradition, but I feel that fusion is a representation of me, and I hope people don't think of me as a disgrace," Alana jokes. "Fusion is a reflection of changing times as our world becomes more interconnected. It is not straying from the past, but building on top of it. Who says we can't create traditions of our own?" –Alana Chandler

But Alana wants young chefs to know that all cooks make mistakes.

Alana is currently majoring in materials science and engineering at MIT, and she encourages you to put on your "metaphorical lab coat." When experimenting, she says it's important to keep track of what components of the recipe you decide to change, whether it be the heat of the oven, how much you knead the dough, or the ratio of wet to dry ingredients. "If you create a recipe that doesn't turn out the best, make sure not to change 30 variables all at once when 'debugging,' because if it comes out bad again, you won't know what went wrong in the original recipe."

Alana reminds you that when you are looking at a picture in a cookbook, these recipes have been perfected many times.

> **ALANA'S RECIPE CREATION PROCESS**
> "It's just a process of research, trial and error, and then a lot of taste testing. Get your family to taste it, give some criticism, and then eventually you'll have a top-notch recipe."

"My first batch of granola came out of the oven charred black," she says. "Where did I go wrong?"

But she kept trying, and eventually she was able to sell her granola.

Cooking is still an important part of Alana's life. "I think my deepest connection to Judaism is probably through food," she says. "Each ingredient carries its own history. A dish is its own novel."

DIJ | DO IT JEWISH
COOKING POSSIBILITIES

1. Take charge at high holiday dinners. "Everyone loves a nice Rosh Hashanah or Yom Kippur break fast, so… maybe ask your parents to scoot over a little bit, so that you can get your hands in the mix." For Alana, that began with her begging if she could "make a dessert instead of my parents buying from a local bakery."

2. Document family recipes. Write them down and take pictures like Jeffrey did with his grandmother's strudel recipe.

3. Look up Jewish food blogs and family cookbooks and see what recipes they have as a source of inspiration.

4. When you eat a Jewish recipe you really love, think how you can put your own "personal spin on it." One starting point Alana suggests is starting with an ingredient you really like. "I'm obsessed with matcha," says Alana, so she's always thinking how she might incorporate it in her recipes.

5. "Don't be afraid to go and interview community members," says Alana. "Learn from as many people as you can because there's not just one best matzoh ball soup when everyone and their mother claim to have the best recipe." Alana encourages you to learn from "multiple number ones, so you can create your own version of number one."

COOKING TOOLS:

* the internet
* Jewish food blogs
* a good knife
* a cutting board
* family cooking tools
* stories from friends and family

6. Alana reminds you to taste even your bad recipes. "As terrible as it is, you've got to put it in your mouth and really try and analyze. What about this tastes off? Is it too chewy? How does it feel against the roof of my mouth? Is it too salty? Is the baking soda making your tongue burn?" She reminds you to look into the food science as well. "Why is this so crumbly?... Adding fats is something that makes recipes moist. Then, you might add more oil to this."

GLOSSARY

Ashkenazi – a Jew whose family and/or traditions came from Eastern Europe

challah – braided egg bread, traditionally made for and eaten on Shabbat

gefilte fish – traditional Jewish fish dish, made from a mixture of fish

kreplach – a Jewish dumpling with meat or other fillings, often served in soup

matcha – finely ground green tea leaves

melon pan – sweet bread covered in a thin layer of cookie crust, traditional in Japan

Rosh Hashanah – the Jewish New Year

Shabbat – a weekly Jewish holiday, the seventh day, a day of rest

Sukkot – a Jewish holiday celebrated by building an outdoor hut called a sukkah

tzimmes – traditional Ashkenazic sweet carrot stew

tzevayim – the Hebrew word for colors, and the name of Alana's cookbook

Yom Kippur – Day of Atonement, a Jewish fast day

JEWISH SONGWRITING

GETTING STARTED

Eliana Light began making up her first songs when she was still a young child.

"Whenever I was left alone, I would sing to myself… and it became a comforting mechanism. Singing about whatever was on my mind or whatever I saw in the world. And that kind of developed into making up songs."

When Eliana was six years old, she would play a game with a friend where they would each give each other a genre and a topic and make up a song. "It was pretty robust, but it was just my way of expressing myself," she says with a laugh.

But how can you get started with your Jewish songwriting?

Eliana explains that your Jewish songwriting can start with an idea, with a feeling, with a prayer, or with an experience.

Eliana encourages using your own experiences and feelings. No one else can write what you write and how you write it

If it's a song for t'filah, Eliana says that it often comes from her just starting to sing it as she prays. "What is the song that my heart wants to sing right now?" asks Eliana.

Sometimes, though, she approaches it differently. Instead of the words speaking to her, she will go looking for the music. "Like wouldn't it be great if we had a new melody for Psalm 96."

Other times, Eliana challenges herself to write songs on a theme. Eliana's second album is all about Jewish ritual objects. So she made a list of objects, and it took a couple of years, but she ended up writing all those songs.

> *What Jewish topic, prayers, places and experiences might inspire your Jewish songs?*

Do I Need To Play An Instrument?

You might think you need to play an instrument to write a song. If you do play guitar or piano, terrific! But even if you don't, you can still write a song.

Eliana didn't play her songs on an instrument when she got started. "I just remembered the melodies that I wrote," she says. "It was just very vivid in my head... how it was on the radio."

Do get a special notebook, just for your songwriting ideas. By fourth grade, Eliana began writing all her songs down. She still has a binder and she still remembers how to sing those songs, including some Jewish ones.

Once you are ready to sing a song you wrote, it is helpful to have a recording device. This can help capture all your song ideas and melodies.

Which Comes First The Lyrics Or The Melody?

Eliana says that for her they often come at the same time. Other times, "I'll sing a line and I'll just start jotting down what comes next.

"Once you have words down on paper, you can start to polish them up to make them as good as can be."

Feel free to explore what works best for you. Most of all, be patient with yourself and enjoy the creative process.

DOING IT JEWISH

So, how do you find an idea for writing your Jewish song?

One good first step to creating good music is getting to know the music that's around you. "If you go to a synagogue," says Eliana, "pay attention to the way certain melodies make you feel.

"There are so many melodies for each of the prayers and each melody is trying to get you to feel a different feeling..."

Eliana has other ideas, too. "Do some research into an area of Jewish wisdom or life you are not so familiar with," suggests Eliana. "If you want to write a song about a holiday, you don't just have to go off what you already know about the holiday. Learn more about it."

Ask yourself, "What is something that I can learn from this prayer that can make me a more open-hearted, kind, or just person?"

Whatever your answer is—use it in your songwriting!

Eliana reminds us that the words of our songs are important. Because our prayers are often translated as "Blessed are you, O Lord," she got it in her head that "God was a big dude in the sky with a beard, zapping people if they did the wrong thing…

"And so I think as a songwriter I recognize that words matter a lot." In her G!D project, Eliana strives "to call out to the mystery of the word *G!d* even if we're not sure what it means."

Eliana feels blessed to be part of "this incredible chain of Jewish songwriters." She explains that "shir" in Hebrew means song and poem, and we have been "shir" writers since the splitting of the sea.

Eliana strives to write songs that "have messages of loving yourself and accepting yourself and loving others and accepting others."

What feelings do you want to share in your Jewish songs?

KEEPING IT GOING

Now that you have lots of ideas flowing and melodies humming through your mind, what next? Will the song just pour out of you, ready to perform?

"You've got to write a lot of bad songs before you can write a good song," Eliana reminds us. She was once in a songwriting workshop with Julie Silver, an amazing Jewish musician, and Julie told them, "I want you to write a bad song."

"We were all kind of stunned," says Eliana. "What do you mean you want us to write a bad song?"

But… "The song I wrote in that workshop is 'The Yad Song,' which is on my second album, which I love.

"Having the freedom to write a bad song—all the pressure being off was really helpful."

Some songs will come easier than others. When Eliana was in fourth grade, she composed her own Modeh Ani. At that time, Doug Cotler, a Jewish musician, came to her synagogue and they gave her a private meeting with him. And he was trying to play music with her song. It was frustrating to her because she could hear the music in her head, but she couldn't translate it for him to play. ("I knew there was a steel drum solo, but there weren't any steel drums," she says.)

Even now, Eliana says that sometimes her songs seem to come out fully formed, but other times it's not so easy. "There are songs that I've been playing around with in my head for years that I have like lines here and lines there, and they haven't become anything yet. Some songs take 20 years to write."

Eliana says to remind yourself, "I can do this… And I can do this in my way." She even suggests stepping away from your work sometimes. "Sleep on it and come back." Don't get frustrated with yourself. It's creativity!

What Is Eliana's Process?

"I'll make a voice recording and then I'll come back to it later…

"If I keep singing it over and over again, if it gets stuck in my head, then it's probably going to get stuck in someone else's. So if you find yourself humming your own tunes, then like, that's pretty good!"

Once Eliana wanted to write a song for Shavuot. She wanted to write a song for kids about the Jewish people at Mount Sinai receiving the Torah. It took a while to get the lyrics right, but once she was able to express her ideas through her song, she knew it was a success.

Another time, though, Eliana was going to write a song for every blessing in the weekday Amidah. "That didn't pan out," she said. But two of the songs she wrote ended up on another of her albums, *s*ngs ab-ut g?d.*

Play around with your lyrics and melodies, suggests Eliana. Don't feel stuck just because you created a song one way.

If you are struggling with writing a song that rhymes, Eliana reminds you to check out a rhyming dictionary or website

And if you are trying to write a rhyming song, she says you can "change the wording around of the first line so that a different word is at the end. If it makes sense and fits with what you are trying to say, do it! If not, try it again."

> *"Music can permit us to sing out. The permission to use our true voices, express the deepest parts of our heart."*
> *—Eliana Light*

Most important of all? Your Jewish songs should reflect you. Being authentically you is what will make your Jewish songs special and unique.

MAKING IT AS GOOD AS IT CAN BE

As a Jewish songwriter, what if you want your Jewish songs to be deeper and more meaningful?

As you write, Eliana suggests paying attention to how your songs make you feel. How could these feelings relate to a Jewish thought or experience?

"It would be cool for you to start noticing that this version of Mi Chamocha makes me feel happy. Oh, maybe that's like the happiness of freedom! But another version may come off a little slower. Maybe it's more like the fear we felt as we were walking through the Red Sea."

When you listen to your songs, you will hear if a word or sound doesn't fit, and then you can revise. Is a line too long? Do you need a different word? Another beat?

Once you have written your song, recorded it, refined it, and recorded it again, it's time to share with people you trust… if you want to.

It's okay to create songs just for yourself, but if you want to take your songs to the next level, feedback can be helpful.

Eliana suggests asking a family member, a good friend, or a teacher for feedback. Let them know exactly what you want them to share in their critique. Does the song make them feel something? Learn something? Want to clap along?

Listen to their feedback. Write down what they say. You might not agree with their critique. Sometimes, the comments that don't make sense WILL make sense later, says Eliana. Just like you need to step away from a song you are working on, review the comments after a few days. You don't have to change anything about your song… but you might want to.

It's not easy to share your work, but taking the risk could help you make your Jewish songs even better.

TAKING IT FURTHER

Once your Jewish song is as good as you know how to make it, what can you do with it? So many things!

Eliana suggests finding other creative people in your school. Are there other kids you know (or don't know yet!) who also enjoy music? Singers, poets, musicians? If you don't play an instrument, maybe you can partner with someone who does and they can accompany you.

Eliana loves working with musicians who are more advanced than she is and who have a better mind for arrangement because then it does end up sounding better. She even sees her relationship with her producer as "almost like hevruta study partners.

"We're not just there to say yes to what each other says. We're there to challenge each other and say, well, what if you tried it like this? What about this instrument? What about changing this one little thing, and the melody and the music ends up being more powerful.

"You can learn a lot from others who may have more knowledge and experience," she says.

Want to take collaboration to the next level? Eliana asks, "What would it be like for you to organize an open mic for everybody just to share in a nonjudgmental love?" Make sure your event is friendly. "Set some ground rules at the beginning, like this is a place where we feel free to express ourselves and to try things without being left out, without feeling bad about ourselves and each other."

What better way to share the Jewish songs you have created?

Eliana Light is a singer, songwriter, educator, and spiritual leader, and creator of THE G!D PROJECT. She is a graduate of the Davidson School at the Jewish Theological Seminary with a Masters in Jewish Experiential Education. She also earned an undergraduate degree in Sociology from Brandeis University. Eliana currently lives in Durham, North Carolina.

"MOM, I HAVE THIS IDEA... I WANT TO START A LADINO ROCK BAND."

– Sarah Aroeste, Ladino singer-songwriter

When Sarah Aroeste was a small child, she could never not be humming. "In the car, in my house, in my bedroom," Sarah laughs.

Now, even when Sarah is not in "songwriting mode," she is still humming. "I have a habit of carrying my phone and having it set to the digital recorder."

Sarah has "hundreds of… ten-second ditties in [her] voice recording app.

"That's just my process," she says. "If I have a tune or a thought that has to come out, I record it."

PASSION FOR LADINO

When Sarah was a junior at Yale, she auditioned for the Israel Vocal Arts Institute, an opera training program in Tel Aviv, and got in.

Sarah grew up hearing Ladino songs in her family. By coincidence, Sarah's coach in Tel Aviv, Nico Castel, happened to be one of the world's leading Ladino experts.

He "was one of the first people to publish a popular songbook in Ladino," exclaims Sarah, and the music "blew my mind"!

When Sarah returned home, she did recitals of classical opera with some Ladino songs. "After every recital," says Sarah, "audience members would…

tell me that the Ladino portion was their favorite.

"Within two or three years, I realized that opera music was not my passion, Ladino music was," she says. "Ultimately I made the switch.

MAKING LADINO MUSIC HER OWN

"I want to start a Ladino rock band," Sarah told her surprised mom.

"There were some wonderful musicians out there doing traditional Ladino music," explains Sarah, "and I loved it, but [the traditional style] wasn't right for me.

"I knew if I was going to… make a go of it doing Ladino music, I needed to do it my own way."

And Sarah's own way was Ladino rock music. She even composed her own original Ladino feminist rock song to thank 15th-century Sephardic heroine Doña Gracia Naci. Naci was like Harriett Tubman, explains Sarah, in her brave efforts to help Crypto—Jews escape the Inquisition.

WHY IS LADINO IMPORTANT?
"It's amazing to me that more people don't know about [Ladino]… It's the best of all these European languages… thrown into one. And it's gorgeous. I mean… it's beautiful to listen to. So, like the actual language itself, I just think is wicked cool."
–Sarah Aroeste

WRITING LADINO KIDS' SONGS

Sarah also loves kids' music, but she couldn't find kids' songs that represented her Sephardic heritage.

So she thought: "I'm a songwriter. I'm just going to write the music myself."

All of the songs on Sarah's first kids' album, *Ora de Despertar* - Time to Wake Up! were inspired by her daughters.

One rhythm was inspired by watching her older daughter walk on the grass barefoot for the first time. "I recorded… watching her feet toddle and that's the rhythm of that song."

SONGWRITING PROCESS

Sometimes Sarah starts with the melody. She listens to those ditties on her voice recorder and thinks, "That could be a song."

Then she thinks, "What kind of song? What kind of lyrics? What kind of feeling do I get from that melody?"

Other times, Sarah starts with an idea. For instance, for each song on her album *Ora de Despertar – Time to Wake Up!*, she wrote the concept first and then translated it into Ladino.

"Writing in another language is complicated," explains Sarah.

"Some of my proudest songs are the ones I that I have actually rhymed in English and Ladino."

Sarah has mentors who are native Ladino speakers. She always sends them her song drafts for review before she publishes anything.

Then Sarah works with her arranging partner to decide what instruments would sound best with her words and melody. They keep adding instruments until they are ready for Sarah to record her vocals.

When it comes to writing music, Sarah wants you to know: "If you do read music and you do know theory, great, but you do not need that to be a songwriter."

In fact, two artists Sarah admires very much don't know how to read music at all.

Sarah recalls her creative, joyful young self: "When I was a four- or five-year-old kid humming all the time, I didn't know how to read music… I just sang."

> SARAH'S CREATIVITY ADVICE:
> "Take risks. Be bold. Find what is unique to you… Don't try to be someone else. You do you. That's what's going to set you apart."

DIJ | DO IT JEWISH
SONGWRITING POSSIBILITIES

1. Use a well-loved song like "Hine Ma Tov" and create a new melody for it. Even though there are many versions of this song, Eliana asks, "Why shouldn't the world have yours, also?"

2. Is there a piece of Jewish wisdom, Jewish life, Jewish teaching that you want to share? Try writing it as a song, suggests Eliana.

3. Use a family memory to start a song. Do you have a favorite food? Do you have a favorite custom? Do you have a favorite object? ("The tiniest little thing can spark a big idea," says Sarah.) So you don't need to start with these huge momentous topics. Start small with something that's really unique to you and use that as your springboard.

4. Create a list of Jewish items or Jewish experiences. Challenge yourself to write a song about all the different items on your list.

5. Keep a recording device handy. Record any tune or ideas that pop into your mind.

SONGWRITING TOOLS:

* a notebook

* a pen

* a recording device

* family photos

* family interviews

GLOSSARY

Amidah – a Jewish prayer that is recited while standing

Crypto-Jews – someone who secretly practices Judaism while officially converting

hevruta – a study pair, traditionally for Jewish subjects

Ladino – Judeo-Spanish, a language traditionally spoken by Sephardic Jews

lyrics – the words to a song

melody – a satisfying sequence of musical notes

Mi Chamocha – a song that was sung after the Israelites safely crossed the Red Sea, a Jewish prayer

Modeh Ani – a prayer that is traditionally sung upon waking up in the morning

Mount Sinai – the mountain where the Torah was received by the Israelites

Psalm – a poem that praises G!d

Sephardic – Jews from Spain and their descendants

Shavuot – the Jewish holiday that celebrates receiving the Torah

shir – song

t'filah – prayer

Torah – sacred text and scroll, the Hebrew Bible

yad – a special pointer used to point when reading the Torah

JEWISH PAINTING & ART

GETTING STARTED

Do you like the idea of creating a Jewish painting that tells a special story? Perhaps it could tell a story about you, your family, or your community?

"Life is art and art is life. So if you're Jewish and you believe in your Jewishness, then you have to believe in the fact that art is a part of that Jewish life," says artist Siona Benjamin.

Siona grew up in Bombay, India, in the Bene Israel community. "India has always been a place where it has accepted people from all over the world… very multicultural and open."

As a result of growing up in such a welcoming community, Siona's art is influenced by her Jewish background, but also by "the world of Hinduism, Islam, Buddhism, Zoro-astrianism, all of these different religions that surrounded" her.

All of the art forms Siona creates are a celebration of both Jewish life and the universality of all people.

Siona has been making art since she was a child. Her parents encouraged her artistic pursuits. She especially loved drawing, and the best gift ever was a "box of markers or a box of paintbrushes."

Learning about color was important for Siona. She remembers her excitement to discover that "primary colors give you secondary colors, and secondary colors give you tertiary colors, and tertiary mixed colors give you quaternary colors."

All through school, Siona's goal was to attend art school in Mumbai. She says, "That's all I knew I wanted to do. There was no other choice for me. I never thought about anything else."

Do you love to draw, paint, and play with color like Siona? Then you can begin creating your own one-of-a-kind Jewish art.

> *"When you're an artist, it's about perseverance."*
> *—Siona Benjamin*

DOING IT JEWISH

Through her paintings, Siona takes her personal stories and "makes them universal." She says, "That's the key."

Most of Siona's paintings portray blue figures. Many of her collections feature biblical characters. Siona uses a paint called gouache, acrylic, and gold leaf in her paintings.

One painting in Siona's "Finding Home" collection is called "Tikkun ha-Olam." It features a blue woman with her many arms, reaching out to create a menorah. The candle-holders are hamsas, and other religious and cultural symbols embellish the painting.

Some of Siona's paintings even feature Jewish superheroes. In one 12-foot-tall installation, Siona created a superhero-style portrait of Lilith. In the painting, Lilith is blue and she is surrounded by fiery color, as she closes her eyes in prayer.

Art by Siona Benjamin

Why Are Siona's Characters Blue?

"Blue is the color of the sky and the ocean… I can belong everywhere and nowhere at the same time… the color of the sky here in America is no different from the color of the sky across the entire world," Siona says. "It's a blue of universality. Anybody can be blue, right?"

Think about a painting or drawing you could create that reflects your unique Jewish environment. What details can you use that are specific to your life? What colors might you use in your painting to convey your ideas and feelings?

A documentary film, *Blue Like Me: The Art of Siona Benjamin*, was created about Siona's art after she received a Fulbright India–US Fellowship. For the fellowship, Siona created a collection of 40 photo-collage paintings called "Faces: Weaving Indian Jewish Narratives."

For this project, Siona did research and conducted interviews with the people she photographed. She explains, "I took these beautiful photographs and then... cut them out on the computer with the help of my assistant." She then layered the portraits with other photographs and images that reflected the life stories of each person portrayed. Finally, she painted and drew on the collages.

Each one of the photo-collages is unique and deeply personal.

One is a group portrait that features the shamash lamplighters from Mumbai synagogues. These three men make sure the flames for the Ner Tamid never go out. Their portrait shows the men surrounded by lamps, embellished with an intricate dancing flame.

Art by Siona Benjamin

Another portrait is of Samson Solomon (Korlekar). He has translated Hebrew prayer books into Marathi so they are accessible to the Jewish community in India. Samson is blind, but is photographed holding a prayer book. There is a look of peace and joy on his face. Siona explains that Samson knows the prayers "almost by heart." Samson's portrait is framed in Jewish symbols and collaged transliterated prayers that decrease in size like an eye examination chart. Photos of his wife, Diana, who assists Samson with his work, also frame the piece.

Maybe you already have some photos saved from a holiday or Hebrew school event that you can turn into beautiful art. Can you interview someone in a photo you took? How could you embellish or decorate a photo to help tell the story of your Jewish family or community?

Another meaningful and unique project Siona designed is a 16-foot circular ceramic tile floor for a synagogue in St. Louis, Missouri. The circular shape was inspired by a mandala. It features depictions of the 12 tribes of Israel, the cycle of Jewish holidays, Zodiac positions, and more. The detailed design also includes some hidden images of moons, faces, and other symbols.

Siona worked with the rabbi to create the floor, "doing sketches back and forth and then… making a final design." Siona did a painting that was converted into large tiles. The tiles were then installed to create the floor. The floor is used as a teaching tool for the synagogue.

What Jewish art could you create for your home or synagogue? What traditions, holidays, or Jewish symbols would you include?

KEEPING IT GOING

Siona's Jewish art is deeply personal. It reflects her life experience, her religious background, and her own belief system.

If you want to create meaningful work, Siona advises you to find inspiration in something personal. She suggests you have fun "finding out who you are, looking into your family background, finding pictures, hearing stories." Siona says that discovering family stories and memorabilia could be the start of an "interesting journey" to making art.

Talk to your parents about your family history. Find out the stories of your grandparents and great-grandparents or other family members.

How will your newly discovered family stories and other treasures inspire you?

Siona recommends you visit museums, art fairs, and events. And explore art books. Be aware of your environment, and always be patient with the process.

> *"Art is not just a luxury, but it's a necessity to… feed the soul."*
> *—Siona Benjamin*

MAKING IT AS GOOD AS IT CAN BE

Going deeper in your work can mean polishing your technique or deepening the connections in your Jewish art projects.

Siona described her process of reading, taking notes, studying, and more. Once she understands the story, she makes sketches to help her "formulate ideas about what she wants to say." She repeats the sketching process, rejecting some ideas as she works until her ideas are finalized.

It's okay when a project doesn't work out right away. Don't get discouraged.

"You have to start somewhere and you have to actually do it." When you do the work, Siona says, "You learn the meaning of… what it is to enjoy the flow of creativity."

TAKING IT FURTHER

If you are interested in being a serious art student, finding a good teacher can help take your work to the next level. Your teacher should be supportive and encouraging.

It is important to keep working on your art. Don't say "I've done enough work!" after only a couple of drawings. Create a portfolio of your work. "Students who persevere in their art," Siona says, "really understand the meaning of the process."

Tikkun Olam and Art

Another way of taking your art to a higher level is to see your creative work as important in the world.

Siona says, "Understanding that my art-making is kind of like tikkun olam, where I can, in my own small way… make meaningful images of the fragments of what's broken out there to put together, to be able to create a form of art that would be helpful. That would be my drop in the ocean of contribution to the world through my art."

Know the impact of your art! What will your "drop in the ocean" be?

Siona Benjamin is an artist and popular speaker. Her multicultural art reflects her Bene Israel community in India as well as her life in America. Siona incorporates cultural and religious symbols in her work, which appears in galleries and museums worldwide. Siona is the recipient of two Fulbright Fellowships, one to India and a second to Israel. Siona's acclaimed art has appeared in numerous publications.

Siona received an MFA in painting from Southern Illinois University-Carbondale, and an MFA in theater set design from the University of Illinois-Urbana/Champaign. Blue Like Me: The Art of Siona Benjamin, a documentary film, was released in 2015.

"THE FACT THAT IT DOESN'T EXIST...
THAT JUST MEANS THAT I SHOULD DO IT."

— Hillel Smith, artist

Four-year-old Hillel Smith went to a birthday party. Everyone else worked on macaroni picture frames and went to the playground when they were finished. Hillel spent the entire party working on his frame.

"I think that's when my parents knew I was going to be an artist," says Hillel.

In college, Hillel explored all kinds of techniques and media that he didn't know existed before.

"That was when I first got into graphic design and silkscreen and large-scale installation projects," says Hillel.

Hillel grew up in an involved Jewish family. He went to a Jewish school and Jewish summer camp and youth group. But he never really saw the art part and the Jewish part as overlapping.

After college, Hillel discovered spray paint stenciling. One day, he decided to spray paint a piece that had Hebrew in it.

One of the friends he showed it to was a curator. "This is so unique… this is what you should be focusing on," said his friend.

"Before, my thinking was that I couldn't do Jewish art in the style that I wanted to do because it didn't exist," says Hillel, but he now realized that the fact that it "doesn't exist doesn't mean anything. That just means that I should do it."

HIS FIRST MURAL

One summer, Hillel was asked to teach ceramics at a local camp.

At their meeting, the director told him, "I actually don't want you to teach ceramics—I saw your spray paint art and want you to teach spray paint."

Hillel never even thought that was something you could teach kids but said, "Let's do it!"

And so, for two summers, he taught spray paint at a camp in Southern California.

Then they said, "We have this handball court. It's kind of ugly. Can you paint a mural on it?"

All Hillel's life he had loved murals. But it had never occurred to him that painting a mural was something that he would do.

Hillel loved painting the mural. He loved working at scale and making huge projects.

Soon Hillel began creating many Jewish murals. In fact, now Jewish art is his career. "It's everything I do now."

Art by Hillel Smith

MANY KINDS OF ART

Among his projects, Hillel has illustrated several Haggadot and created a book of parsha posters. ("What if I designed posters advertising the Torah portion for Shabbat?" he asked himself.)

And each year, he creates a very special shalach manot container for Purim. While many people use a simple bag or basket, Hillel considers shalach manot to be "an amazing package design exercise."

Hillel enjoys setting limitations on the projects he makes. "These boxes had to be made from one sheet of paper and no more. No glue or staples… and no printing," he says. "So it's just paper cut up in different ways and folded and repositioned."

He finds these restrictions boost his creativity.

For last year's container, he was inspired by intricate lattice windows. He even put little lights inside so the words "Happy Purim" appear in the shadows.

"Engaging in Jewish art is how we should be engaging with Judaism. Adding life and energy and meaning to all of the things that we do throughout the Jewish day, the Jewish week, our Jewish life, and in every holiday and ritual that we have."
–Hillel Smith

A JEWISH STREET ART FESTIVAL

Many Jewish schools and Jewish Community Centers have commissioned Hillel to create a mural.

He has to sketch and plan carefully to make sure that he will have enough time (and paint) to complete the mural while he is on site at their location.

And in a mural, "an individual letter could be five feet tall," so he says, "Ignore the voice in your head. Trust the measurements."

Hillel was excited to discover that there were other artists creating large Jewish murals. Eventually, he planned the Jewish Street Art Festival.

The 10 festival artists painted 18 murals in three locations around Jerusalem.

Hillel tried to bring typography into his pieces. Another artist brought in her Syrian heritage. And one artist brought her grandfather's poetry into her work.

Hillel loved creating a festival with "all of these artists… [with] all kinds of different backgrounds from all across the world… to say there are so many different ways to be Jewish."

DIJ | DO IT JEWISH
PAINTING & ART POSSIBILITIES

1. Create your own shalach manot container for Purim like Hillel does. Will you use the same "rules" that he does or will you create some of your own?

2. Create a photo collage like Siona has done of an important Jewish person in your life. How can you use your illustrations to enhance the photo and show that person practicing their Judaism?

3. Create a painting to reflect your unique Jewish environment. Think carefully about the colors you choose.

4. Think big and create your own Jewish mural! Don't paint on a wall unless you have permission. (See Hillel's great ideas for alternative surfaces below!)

PAINTING & ART TOOLS:
* paint brushes
* paints to experiment with could include: watercolors, acrylics, gouache, colored ink, paint pens, pastels, and more
* spray ink
* sketchbook
* paper or canvas

* possible mural surfaces: plywood, lauan, masonite, unmounted canvas or, for a temporary mural, plastic mounted between two trees

Please note: Hillel explains that spray paint is for ages 10 and up, with adult supervision only. And you must use appropriate safety gear, including a respirator, goggles, gloves, and sunscreen

GLOSSARY

Fulbright India-US Fellowship – a program whose goal is to promote intercultural relations

graphic design – communicating visually, using typography, photographs, and more

Haggadot – the plural of Haggadah (a special book used for Passover)

hamsa – a traditional symbol of a hand

installation projects – an art piece that you build so people can immerse themselves inside

Lilith – a powerful female in Jewish mythology, Adam's first wife

Marathi – one of many languages spoken in India

menorah – a candelabrum with seven or nine lamps, originally used in the Temple

ner tamid – eternal light in the synagogue

parsha – the weekly Torah portion

Purim – a Jewish holiday where we dress up in costumes and read the book of Esther

Shabbat – a weekly Jewish holiday, the seventh day, a day of rest

shalach manot – traditional Purim gifts of food, delivered in a basket or other container

shamash – traditional lamplighters of the eternal light, also the candle that lights the other candles on Hanukkah

silkscreen – a stencil printing technique that pushes ink through a screen onto a surface beneath

tikkun olam – the Jewish concept of repairing the world

typography – the art of designing letters and fonts, and arranging text on the page

MAKING MIDRASH

GETTING STARTED

If you like reading and writing Jewish stories, you will enjoy learning more about midrash and maybe even writing your own.

What is midrash, exactly?

A midrash is a creative work based on a Bible story that adds more details, a new perspective, or interprets the traditional story in a new way.

Rabbi Sandy Eisenberg Sasso, an award-winning author of children's books, explains that midrash is a "classical tradition in Judaism," a way of filling in the blank spaces in biblical stories.

Rabbi Sasso wanted to be a writer since she was in middle school, even before she wanted to become a rabbi. As a rabbi, storytelling became an important way for her to connect with children. Storytelling through midrash is a perfect blending of Judaism and writing.

Many of Rabbi Sasso's books are midrash, like *Noah's Wife: The Story of Naamah*. We all know about

Noah building an ark to save all the animals during a flood. But when a young student asked Rabbi Sasso, "Who is Noah's wife?" she didn't have an answer. That sparked an idea. Rabbi Sasso "filled in the blank spaces," and created a midrash about Naamah.

Why is midrash important?

Rabbi Sasso emphasizes that our tradition is not meant to be frozen in time. "It is alive. And if it's alive, then you are part of it and you are continuing to create it like I have."

She elaborates, "Judaism isn't just the voice of the past, it's the voice of many pasts layered upon one another. Now, we too can add our voices."

So you can add your midrash voice to the voices of the past, just like Rabbi Sasso has done.

DOING IT JEWISH

"At the core of being a Jew is to ask a question," Rabbi Sasso says. Once you have chosen a Bible story or character to explore, like she chose Noah's wife, ask yourself questions:

* "What would I want to know that the story is not telling me?"
* "Whose voice is not heard?"
* "Is there something missing from the story?"
* "How would I feel if I were in a similar situation?"

Also, Rabbi Sasso says, imagine being one of the characters in your midrash. "Have the silent characters speak. Have them talk to each other."

When Rabbi Sasso wrote *Noah's Wife: The Story of Naamah*, she invented conversations between Noah and Naamah, and between Naamah and the raven, to help develop the story.

Can you picture the days of creation in your mind? Imagine playing music with Miriam? Crossing the Red Sea with Moses?

There are so many wonderful Bible stories with interesting characters.

Which one will you choose?

KEEPING IT GOING

Once you have chosen a Bible story and compiled your questions, it is time to dig in!

Learn all you can about your Bible story and the characters involved. An online search or a visit to the library will help you find resources, both old and new. Rabbi Sasso says you may even find inspiration in an artwork of your Bible story. Research is like a treasure hunt. You are sure to find some gems to help you create a midrash with your own flavor.

But how does research help you create midrash?

Before Rabbi Sasso wrote about Naamah, she found existing text that said Naamah's "deeds were pleasing." Then, she found a reference calling her "Emzera, Mother of Seed."

These two nuggets of information fit together like puzzle pieces for Rabbi Sasso. In her mind, she "knew" Naamah. And her story began to take shape. "She [Naamah] took the seeds of every plant and she planted them on the ark. And after the flood, she replanted the earth's garden."

Then Rabbi Sasso took her research to the next level. She spoke with botanists and learned about categorizing plants. As the story unfolded, questions about Naamah came up like "How does she carry all the plants?" Rabbi Sasso resolved this by giving Naamah an apron with many pockets where she could carry seeds and plants. A perfect solution!

Including specific details like Rabbi Sasso did with Naamah's many-pocketed apron can help make your midrash more interesting to your readers.

MAKING IT AS GOOD AS IT CAN BE

Before you start writing your midrash, Rabbi Sasso has some reminders:

"If you are going to make a story, you have to have three-dimensional characters. You have to have a beginning, a middle, and an end." Also, she says, every story should have a problem, a conflict, and a solution to the conflict.

During the writing process, "give yourself time," says Rabbi Sasso. She encourages you to go to a deep place when you want to create (or read) a midrash. "If you really want to get to a deep place," she says, "you have to turn off the sound because you're never going to listen to what's inside of you.

"And give yourself permission to make mistakes." Keep working to refine your midrash. Your first draft will not be the same as your final one.

"Writing is work. But I love that kind of work. I love the process of creating characters, putting sentences together, developing a rhythm."
—Rabbi Sandy Eisenberg Sasso

As you work through your midrash, you may get stuck. That means you've run out of ideas or inspiration. Don't give up! Even Rabbi Sasso gets frustrated sometimes. "Move away from what you're doing for a while," she says. Take time for other activities you enjoy. A new idea may surprise you when you least expect it.

So, once you have written your midrash, revised it, stepped away from your work, and perhaps revised again, what's next?

Feedback can help you refine your midrash. Read it out loud. And when you are ready, share your midrash with friends, family, and even your teachers—with people you trust will take you seriously.

And while it's helpful to know what parts of your midrash your readers question, "Remember, it's your story," Rabbi Sasso advises. You can listen to comments, but you don't have to take every suggestion.

TAKING IT FURTHER

Find ways to share your midrash with a larger circle. Leaders in your synagogue will be delighted to know about your midrash. You can share with your religious school class, too. Rabbi Sasso encourages you to let them all know you have been studying and creating midrash. She says you may even consider submitting your work to a children's magazine. Be proud of your creation!

Once you have written your first midrash, keep going! Keep asking questions and keep creating new midrash.

Rabbi Sasso is always looking for new ways to make Bible stories meaningful. For example, the story of Noah's ark can lead to discussions about environmental disasters. "What makes a tradition continue to live is its ability to continue to hear new voices."

Rabbi Sasso is interested in how the generations have taken sacred stories and "continued to interpret the story in response to what was happening around them and within them."

> *Story allows us not just to know, but to feel.... you get inside people's characters in their hearts and their minds... I think it just enables us to touch on the deeper parts of ourselves. -Rabbi Sandy Eisenberg Sasso*

By creating midrash, you can become part of this important tradition.

A final thought from Rabbi Sasso: Keep all your work, even as you become a more experienced writer. She still has a book that she wrote in school. She says, "It means a lot to me to see where I started and where I'm going."

Remember to celebrate every step of your creative journey!

Sandy Eisenberg Sasso is an award-winning author of numerous children's books. Noah's Wife: The Story of Na'amah was chosen as one of the Best Books of the Year by Publishers Weekly. Other books based on midrash are Cain & Abel – Finding the Fruits of Peace, Adam & Eve's First Sunset, *and* A Very Big Problem *(co-authored with Amy-Jill Levine). Other awards her books have received include the Sugarman Family Children's Book Award, National Jewish Book Award, and Indiana Authors Award, among others. She was also honored with the Helen Keating Ott Award for Outstanding Contribution to Children's Literature. Rabbi Sasso is active in the interfaith community. She serves as the director of the Religion, Spirituality, and the Arts Initiative at the IUPUI Arts and Humanities Institute.*

"WHAT DOES SARAH'S LAUGH LOOK LIKE IN YOUR FINGERTIPS?"

— Rabbi Susan Freeman, dancer with Avodah Dance Ensemble & co-author of *Torah in Motion*

"The whole concept of dance midrash is all about collaboration," emphasizes JoAnne Tucker, founder of the Avodah Dance Ensemble. JoAnne collaborated with Avodah members, among them Kezia Gleckman Hayman, and Rabbi Susan Freeman, to create dance midrash together.

As a child, "I was very much interested in improv and danced around my living room very freely," says Rabbi Freeman.

JoAnne started dancing to her grandmother playing music when she was just two or three. Then she was "very lucky at age six or seven to learn from an excellent teacher who taught creative dance."

"I think I might be a little unusual," says Kezia, "in that I was not particularly creative."

Kezia studied ballet, which is very disciplined. "Within that discipline, I had an ability to be expressive in my own way, but I didn't like to make up my own movements." When Kezia got to college, she found improv classes very difficult because she found it "almost paralyzing to have to come up with something myself."

Kezia emphasizes that it's helpful with any sort of improv work to have some guiding rules. "To create something from scratch was very daunting," she says, "but once I was given a couple of tasks to meet within that improv, I found a freedom to play with those challenges."

"It's within a structure that real creativity happens," agrees JoAnne. "Yes, we can float around and… dance in our living rooms… But the more we begin to structure that, the richer the creativity becomes."

HOW DANCE MIDRASH CAME TO BE

"It began with Rabbi Rick Jacobs, who was a member of the dance company," explains JoAnne. She and Rabbi Jacobs created a dance that was originally in five parts. "The first and the last part worked and the middle was awful."

So they threw out the middle and brainstormed. "Let's do a midrash," they decided.

Their dance midrash would come from that week's Torah portion. "What jumped out at us? What did we want to do?" Sometimes they would let the congregation or the rabbi choose the line they would base their midrash on.

"It was not set choreography," explains JoAnne. "It was created at the spur of the moment in front of the congregation."

"The discovery really happens when you're doing it," adds Kezia.

TORAH IN MOTION

JoAnne and Rabbi Freeman wrote a book together called *Torah in Motion*. Their book shows teachers how to use dance midrash.

"There might be some brainstorming that happens beforehand," explains Rabbi Freeman, so "we would provide some structure for that brainstorm."

If the idea from the Torah was "going forth," they might challenge students to walk across the room and "go forth" in as many ways as they can.

This would help them build their "confidence and competence," she explains. And give them more comfort and ideas when they would get to the "spontaneous improvisational section."

Creativity in Judaism: "One thing about Jewish creativity is that it's built into our whole way of learning over the centuries… The idea that all the different voices [in the Talmud] have a legitimate place on the page… Judaism is very creative at its core by its nature."
–Rabbi Susan Freeman

JoAnne explains that with dance, "you get down to a core place that's deeper than language."

CREATING DANCE MIDRASH

A wonderful drummer that JoAnne and Kezia regularly worked with, including at the Institute for Contemporary Midrash, had "this huge bag of percussion instruments," says JoAnne. So JoAnne began collecting percussion instruments and these became a key part of her workshops.

Searching for Women's Voices in Judaism: "We revisit the biblical Sarah many times to try to find out where we as women fit into Judaism."
–JoAnne Tucker

"If you like materials and costumes, find a costume," says JoAnne. Whatever inspires you!

Kezia finds that it's sometimes easiest to pick "parts of the Torah that have characters in them, especially if they're siblings or families."

She also suggests that if "there are lines in the text that have movement words in them, those are often easier to start with.

"So if there's someone hiding or falling or carrying something or reaching or wrestling…"

And finally: "It's okay to start small," reminds Rabbi Freeman. "A whole big dance is going to be overwhelming, but what does Sarah's laugh look like in your fingertips?

"You could add something small to that and you can put the laugh in a foot and a hand. And then you can put it in your hips…" and soon "you're dancing Sarah's laugh!"

1. Read a story from the Torah. What questions do you have about your story? Try to write a midrash to "fill in the blanks" of the story.

2. Choose a Torah character you don't know much about. Do a bit of research. Then bring the character to life through writing or dancing (or painting) a midrash.

3. Try to create a short dance midrash about a Torah story. What very small aspect of the Torah story will you start with? How can you move your body to bring the Torah to life?

4. Incorporate costumes and/or instruments into your dance midrash.

5. Try to expand your short midrash into a longer story or dance.

MAKING MIDRASH TOOLS:

* a translation of the Torah
* paper and pencil
* your questions and ideas
* instruments
* scarves
* costumes
* anything that inspires you

GLOSSARY

Avodah – the Hebrew word for work or worship

choreography – the steps and moves of a dance

improv – acting or dancing that is not planned but created spontaneously

midrash – a story or other creative art form that fills in the "blank spaces" of a Torah story

percussion – musical instruments that are played by being struck or scraped, includes drums, bells and tambourines

Sarah's laugh – Sarah laughs in the Torah when she hears that she, an elderly woman, will be giving birth

Torah – sacred text and scroll, the Hebrew Bible

CREATING JUDAICA

GETTING STARTED

Judaica refers to the beautiful objects we use to honor and celebrate Jewish life—such as Shabbat candlesticks, kiddush cups, seder plates, and spice boxes for Havdalah. Along with having religious significance, each of these items is a work of art.

Would you like to make a piece of Judaica for your family or a friend? Maybe even for yourself?

Artist Harriete Estel Berman creates beautiful candlesticks, one-of-a-kind detailed seder plates, tzedakah boxes, and more. Her process is unique. So are the materials that she uses. Many years ago, Harriete made the decision to only work with recycled materials.

Her pieces are created out of things like recycled cans, vintage dollhouses, and old metal packaging. By using materials that could be considered waste, Harriete's goal is to "have the least detrimental impact on the world" while helping "people see [the materials] in new ways."

From the time she was a young girl, Harriete wanted to be an artist. She remembers doing lots of art projects when she was growing up. One year for Purim she dressed

"I just could not take new materials any longer to make things."
—Harriete Estel Berman

up like a beatnik, celebrating her creative spirit! In college, she studied metalsmithing and jewelry making. These techniques are the perfect foundation for the Judaica she creates today.

Are you ready to have some creative fun making Judaica with recycled materials?

DOING IT JEWISH

"This is how I observe my Jewishness, by making Judaica," Harriete says about her work.

Harriete began making Judaica when she was invited to create a piece for the Contemporary Jewish Museum in San Francisco. She created a kiddush cup crafted out of recycled blue and white tzedakah boxes.

At first, Harriete wondered how her Judaica from recycled materials would be received. Would museum patrons appreciate her unique materials? Traditionally, kiddush cups are silver, but hers was colorful blue and made of tin. The response was overwhelmingly positive! This gave Harriete the confidence to keep creating Judaica out of recycled materials.

Since that first kiddush cup, Harriete has created many elaborate works, each one handcrafted and one-of-a-kind. All of her Judaica pieces are detailed with meaningful symbolism.

For example, Harriete's series of seder plates are crafted from vintage tin dollhouses. She used the windows from the dollhouses to symbolize how we invite guests into our homes on Passover. The cutout dollhouse doors remind us of welcoming Elijah.

How can you use recycled materials to create Judaica?

First, you need to collect your materials.

One of Harriete's favorite materials to make preliminary models (before cutting metal) is recycled cardboard boxes. She especially loves working with cereal boxes. Harriete says you can go miles with a cereal box! "The great thing about a cereal box is that it already has some folds in it." You can use the folds to create your shape, or you can cut and glue pieces together. Experiment and have fun with your project. If you don't have any cereal boxes, Harriete says cracker boxes work well, too. Get creative! What materials will you make your Judaica out of?

If you don't know what kind of Judaica you'd like to create, Harriete recommends starting out creating your own tzedakah box. Before you know it, the ideas will be flowing! Harriete says to ask your neighbors to save cereal boxes for you. Before long you will have enough for plenty of projects.

KEEPING IT GOING

You will need some tools to make your Judaica.

Harriete uses some pretty heavy-duty tools to cut though metal. But don't worry! There are other, more accessible tools and supplies you can use to create your Judaica.

Some items you might want to gather before you get started: scissors, masking tape, Elmer's glue, hot-glue gun, paint, glitter, any other decorative materials. You probably already have some in your kitchen or craft drawer.

Important Safety Note: Adult supervision required for hot-glue gun usage.

Harriete's work takes a lot of patience, in both planning and creating. She says, "Metalwork itself is so time-consuming–if you put 20 or 30 hours into one element, you've been thinking about it a long time."

Even if you are working with elements like paper, cardboard, and tape, it takes time to create a meaningful piece.

Harriete explains that every project has different phases. It starts with the "idea phase," which passes quickly and is "almost romanticized." Next comes a more challenging awkward phase, when you might have doubts about your project. This phase feels "really long," but Harriete advises you to "push through that place." Don't give up!

MAKING IT AS GOOD AS IT CAN BE

If you aren't happy with the results of your project, it's okay. Harriete says the best part about using recycled materials is that you can start over. "You can do better on the second time," says Harriete. "Every single time you do something again and again and again and again, it's going to get better!"

Harriete advises you to experiment, take risks, and make mistakes! It's all part of the creative process, and according to Harriete, "Super-duper, incredibly important!"

Besides, Harriete says, "Most mistakes can be fixed with paint and glitter!"

TAKING IT FURTHER

Research can take your Judaica to a new level of meaning.

Harriete is very thoughtful about the topics she explores through her art. Harriete created another piece for the Contemporary Jewish Museum in San Francisco. It is a seder plate she calls "Eons of Exodus." She was inspired by images of the biblical exodus from a 1924 Hebrew Union Haggadah her family used when she was growing up.

Making the seder plate was an in-depth process, and it began with research. Harriete wanted to show the exodus of Jews (and others) throughout time. She researched

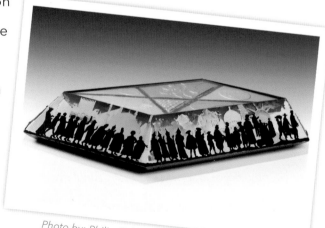

Photo by: Philip Cohen, Copyright: Harriete Estel Berman

historical clothing and architecture, and every detail she needed to create her vision.

Using recycled tin cans, she created silhouette images of the Jewish people walking together, carrying their belongings. The seder plate has images that represent historical costumes of the Jewish people throughout the centuries. Harriete also included images of Japanese Americans at the internment camps, the lost boys of Sudan, and Sudanese women carrying bundles.

"I also think of the seder service as people. We're inside looking out our windows, but people, the stranger on the street, might be looking in at our window."
–Harriete Estel Berman

Using this depth of knowledge and the images she unearthed in her research, Harriete worked tirelessly to create a unique work of Judaica. She says that the "super amazingly difficult part is to take an abstract idea about the exodus or migration of the Jewish people for 2000 years and create that as images," and then decide "how you are going to render that" going around the seder plate.

Harriete needed to make sure the images were just right as they fit around the seder plate, keeping in mind the construction of the background images and the movement of the scenes. She says, "It's very thoughtful, it's very planned out."

Harriete takes us through her artistic thought process. She explains, "I have the bigger ideas and then I have the details. I think the details go back to the very nature of existence as an artist… The details are everything. It's like I cannot make it with less than every single aspect making some contribution to the whole."

Attention to detail "also means the pieces take a really long time because I'm putting a great deal of detail and effort into them and I'm thinking about how every single aspect can have meaning," Harriete says.

A final thought:

According to Harriete, creating Judaica and art from recycled materials is no small undertaking. It is a powerful act of "righteousness and responsibility for our earth."

Tikkun olam, our responsibility to repair the world, can start with art!

Harriete Estel Berman is an award-winning artist. She works with recycled materials to create jewelry, sculptures, and Judaica. Her work appears in numerous permanent museum collections and has been exhibited in the United States, Europe, and Africa. All of Harriete's pieces are infused with social commentary. Harriete earned a BFA from Syracuse University and an MFA from Temple University.

"I AM WRITING... FROM NASA...
AND I WOULD LIKE TO TAKE YOUR APOLLO
MEZUZAH ON THE UPCOMING EXPEDITION."

– as told to Laura Cowan
by astronaut Greg Chamitoff

When she was younger, Laura Cowan's favorite subject in school was art, but her school was "quite old-fashioned and we were only taught still-life drawing and painting."

Laura had never considered art to be anything other than that until she took an art foundation course. This course is a requirement for acceptance into an art degree in the United Kingdom.

"In the foundation course we dabbled in sculpture, ceramics, 3D design, and photography," explains Laura.

By the end of the course, Laura realized that she wanted to work in 3D. "But something commercial," says Laura, "so I decided that jewelry was right for me."

LEARNING TO MAKE JUDAICA

Laura studied silversmithing and jewelry at university. This was a four-year course and included apprenticeships.

Laura also did an apprenticeship in Israel at the Megiddo jewelry factory,

and another internship with the extraordinary glass sculptor Danny Lane.

Her final project was based on the moon landings, and included rocket-shaped necklaces and other objects.

Laura's Judaica has been exhibited at museums all around the world. She has an *Apollo* mezuzah in the Spertus museum in Chicago, a smart dreidel that teaches you how to play the dreidel game in the Jewish Museum in New York, and a moon seder plate in Vienna.

"Each design has a different starting point," explains Laura. "My early collection grew out of a fascination with the moon landings."

Laura is not sure how it started, but she "spent days in the university library reading books about the space race between Russia and America, and following President Kennedy's national goal for the 1960s of 'landing a man on the moon and returning him safely to the earth.'"

Laura's more recent collections have been inspired by Bauhaus architecture in Tel Aviv, and the Sinai's sand dunes.

A MEZUZAH BLASTS OFF

One day, Laura received a mysterious email asking what the exact weight of her *Apollo* mezuzah was.

Then, a few weeks later, she received an email from the NASA astronaut Greg Chamitoff. "I am writing here from NASA Texas," wrote Greg, "and I would like to take your *Apollo* mezuzah on the upcoming *Expedition* 17." He brought two mezuzot with him on the expedition for his friends and colleagues.

Apollo Mezuzah by Laura Cowan

"NASA allows astronauts a [few] items to be flown for other people," explains Laura.

Laura and Greg stayed in touch by email, and when he received his next mission, to the International Space Station, he flew an Apollo mezuzah for Laura and gave it to her when he returned.

"I have it framed in my studio!" exclaims Laura.

Laura's mezuzah in space with astronaut Greg Chamitoff

This was exciting for Laura personally and professionally. There were articles in the Israeli press and Jewish press worldwide. It was even on Russian TV!

WHY JUDAICA MATTERS

Laura makes Judaica "to encourage Jews to connect to their Judaism through attractive, meaningful, modern design." She explains, "This helps us perform mitzvot such as hanging a mezuzah or making kiddush."

Jewish life provides inspiration for Laura's Judaica creations.

"There are so many Jewish holidays and traditions," says Laura. "Each tradition or mitzvah has specific rules and these provide me with an outline for the design.

"I know of customers that, for instance, didn't light Shabbat candlesticks until they were gifted one of my designs."

CREATING DESIGNS OF YOUR OWN

Laura makes her Judaica out of metal, but she emphasizes that that is not the only way. "Silversmithing is a profession that is learned slowly, with a lot of time at the bench; there are no shortcuts. You have to be very dedicated," she says. "But Judaica can also be made from found objects."

Last year, Laura made a hannukiah with her children out of clothespins.

Don't forget to follow the rules of halacha when making your Judaica, says Laura. These are the Jewish laws concerning how to make many of the various Jewish ritual objects.

Finally, she invites you: "Try to create something that hasn't been made before."

> Laura's Creativity Advice: "Open your heart and mind and allow your imagination to run wild!"

DIJ | DO IT JEWISH
CREATING JUDAICA POSSIBILITIES

1. Create your own tzedakah box. Will you use a cereal box or another container to create it? How will you decorate it to make it look as beautiful as possible?

2. Make the most beautiful challah cover you possibly can. Will you paint it, sew it, create a collage? What will you put on your challah cover to make it perfect for Shabbat?

3. Gather found objects and create your own hanukkiah or other one-of-a-kind Judaica item.

4. What Judaica item can you create using only scotch tape, recycled items, and your imagination?

JUDAICA TOOLS:

* recycled materials
* found objects
* art supplies
* scotch tape
* masking tape
* pliers
* your imagination!

GLOSSARY

beatnik – a poetry-reading artist from the 1960s

dreidel – a spinning top with Hebrew letters used to play a game for Hanukkah

Elijah – a prophet; the door is opened for Elijah on Passover

Exodus – leaving Egypt when the Israelites were slaves

halacha – Jewish law

hanukkiah – a Hanukkah menorah

Havdalah – a ritual separating Shabbat from the rest of the week

kiddush – the blessing over the wine

metalsmithing – the skill of creating items out of metal

mezuzah – ritual object that is attached to a doorpost, means "doorpost"

mezuzot – plural of mezuzah

mitzvah – a commandment

mitzvot – plural of mitzvah

Passover – a holiday celebrating the Exodus of the Israelites from ancient Egypt

Purim – a holiday with costumes and reading the book of Esther

seder plate – a plate filled with traditional symbols of Passover

Shabbat – a weekly Jewish holiday, the seventh day, a day of rest

silversmithing – the skill of creating items out of silver

tikkun olam – the Jewish tradition of repairing the world

tzedakah – often means charity, literally means "righteousness"

WHY JEWISH CREATIVITY?

Judaism is filled with creativity. From the very beginnings of Jewish history, there were Jewish artists and creatives. From Miriam and the women who danced and sang joyously with their instruments after crossing the Red Sea to the artisan Bezalel who constructed the intricate Tabernacle the Israelites carried as they wandered through the desert, Jewish creativity has been part of our religion since the very beginning.

In *DIJ—DO IT JEWISH: USE YOUR JEWISH CREATIVITY*, you met a wide array of contemporary Jewish creativity experts. From Jewish cooking to Jewish cartooning and from Jewish filmmaking to creating Judaica, we are thrilled with the incredible range of talented, thoughtful, and reflective individuals who graciously agreed to be a part of these pages.

We hope you enjoyed learning about how these experts expressed their creativity when they were young and how they have dealt with various creative challenges. Each was generous in sharing their Jewish creativity advice with you, the reader, and we welcome you to think of them as your Jewish creativity mentors.

We hope that you consider DIJ as much more than a book. Instead we encourage you to think of these chapters as an invitation. Within them, you can discover an exciting tapestry of ways to express your own unique Jewish creativity. We invite you to experiment, create and explore!

To learn more about Jewish creativity, please visit
www.IntergalacticAfikoman.com.

BARBARA BIETZ is an award-winning author of several books for children. Barbara created the website JewishBooksforKids.com where she interviews authors, illustrators, editors, and more. When Barbara isn't reading, she is probably typing away at her desk working on a manuscript. Barbara loves reading, doing crafts, and playing the guitar. She lives with her family in Southern California. Visit her online at www.BarbaraBietz.com.

DARIA GRINEVICH is passionate about traveling the world. She loves exploring the mystery of new countries through nature, and unfamiliar cultures by living with the locals and learning new languages. One time, she spent a month restoring a castle from the middle ages in France. Ever since childhood, Daria could spend hours on arts and crafts of all kinds and later she graduated with a degree in Architecture and Town Planning. Through her illustrations, Daria gives magical life to everyday objects in her own special vision with different mediums and techniques. You can find her daily sketches and illustrations on her Instagram page, @Darianrty.

With tremendous gratitude, *todah rabah*
to our incredible experts in Jewish creativity:

Sarah Aroeste

Siona Benjamin

Harriete Estel Berman

Alana Chandler

Laura Cowan

Rabbi Susan Freeman

Kezia Gleckman Hayman

Rachel Harrison Gordon

Jordan B. "Gorf" Gorfinkel

Terri Libenson

Eliana Light

Amy Linton

Nora Claire Miller

Peter Miller

Rabbi Sandy Eisenberg Sasso

Hillel Smith

JoAnne Tucker

Jeffrey Yoskowitz

Erez Zadok

Credits

Intergalactic Afikoman thanks all those who graciously gave us permission to share their creativity within these pages. We diligently attempted to secure the necessary permissions to share all copyrighted material. Should there be any inadvertent oversight, we express our deep regret and will be happy to correct it in future editions. Our grateful acknowledgement is made to the following:

JEWISH CRE

understanding your place in this world and how you can
make it better and make yourself better.
   —Rachel Harrison Gordon, creator of BROKEN BIRD

all about asking. Asking different questions.
Looking at this interesting complex process of
storytelling . . . for the future.
   —Nora Claire Miller, creator of EGG CREAM

nurturing my soul.
   —Amy Linton,
editor of EGG CREAM

allowing your mind
to open, to use your
own ideas, and not a
preconceived idea. But
with soul, a respect for
Gd and following the
directives of Halacha.
   —Laura Cowan, artist

taking your imagination and injecting it with your
personal Jewish experiences and beliefs.
   —Terri Libenson, author of BECOMING BRIANNA

something that uses the rituals, the symbols, the traditions, the stories,
the ideas of the Jewish people. It is alive; you are part of it, and you
are continuing to add your story.
   —Rabbi Sandy Eisenberg Sasso, picture book author

let's say our Haggadah is taking an ancient thing that is hard to
understand and making it more engaging with a graphic novel with comics.
   —Erez Zadok , illustrator of PASSOVER HAGGADAH GRAPHIC NOVEL